*For Austin, who will not read this
but will tell everyone I dedicated my book to him.*

*In earnest, thank you for always supporting me, Chip.
Without you, I'd never believe I could.*

Inspiring | Educating | Creating | Entertaining

Brimming with creative inspiration, how-to projects, and useful information to enrich your everyday life, Quarto Knows is a favorite destination for those pursuing their interests and passions. Visit our site and dig deeper with our books into your area of interest: Quarto Creates, Quarto Cooks, Quarto Homes, Quarto Lives, Quarto Drives, Quarto Explores, Quarto Gifts, or Quarto Kids.

© 2021 Quarto Publishing Group USA Inc.
Text © 2021 Robyn Valentine

First Published in 2021 by Fair Winds Press, an imprint of The Quarto Group,
100 Cummings Center, Suite 265-D, Beverly, MA 01915, USA.
T (978) 282-9590 F (978) 283-2742 QuartoKnows.com

Fair Winds Press titles are also available at discount for retail, wholesale, promotional, and bulk purchase. For details, contact the Special Sales Manager by email at specialsales@quarto.com or by mail at The Quarto Group, Attn: Special Sales Manager, 100 Cummings Center, Suite 265-D, Beverly, MA 01915, USA.

25 24 23 22 21   1 2 3 4 5

ISBN: 978-1-58923-993-7

Digital edition published in 2021
eISBN: 978-1-58923-994-4

Library of Congress Cataloging-in-Publication Data is available.

Design: Cindy Samargia Laun
Illustration: Stasia Burrington

Printed in China

MAGICKAL TAROT

SPREADS, SPELLWORK, AND RITUAL FOR CREATING YOUR LIFE

ROBYN VALENTINE
Creator of *Tired Witch*

C**O**NTENTS

INTRODUCTION: TAROT AS A MAGICKAL TOOL

You may know tarot as a tool for divination, but divination is only the beginning of its usefulness. All magickal tools are based on symbolism and are associated with historic knowledge about *why* we use them. Understanding the *why* is vital for all magickal applications, and tarot is no different.

In fact, tarot is chock full of symbolism. With knowledge of this symbolism, you will find that it becomes an easily accessible magickal tool for spellwork, ritual, and beyond. In this book, we will explore the symbolism of the Major Arcana and the energies associated with the cards of the traditional Rider-Waite-Smith deck.

It's important that we give credit to Pamela Colman Smith for the imagery we see in the Rider-Waite-Smith deck, because her name has mostly been forgotten due to her odd (for the times) lifestyle and role in society. Although Waite is credited for the creation of the deck, Smith was the artist behind the imagery we most commonly associate with tarot. During the turn of the last century, it was nearly unheard of to credit a woman of (theorized) mixed-race background, one who may have been LGBTQIA+, for her contributions. For this reason, it is not only important but necessary that we include her today.

Once you have a firm understanding of each card's symbolism, the doors to a countless array of magickal possibilities will open for you!

1

INTRODUCTION TO THE MAJOR ARCANA

The Major Arcana is the set of the first twenty-two cards of any tarot deck that follows the Rider-Waite-Smith formatting. They are the biggest and most impactful cards of a deck. These twenty-two cards represent situations we all face in the grand scheme of life, with each carrying specific messages of perspective and guidance. They follow The Fool's journey through life's social, personal, and emotional issues. As we will see throughout this book, we can also use the Major Arcana as a ritual tool, as the cards are full of symbolism and specific energies.

Prior to the seventeenth century, the Major Arcana card deck was simply a variation of a gaming deck. Although the cards may have held cultural significance, they held little occult or spiritual weight. The symbolism of the cards we discuss throughout this book, the Rider-Waite-Smith deck, was brought to life in the early twentieth century (although it has been reimagined time and time again).

WHY LEARNING SYMBOLISM IS IMPORTANT

Once we learn *why* specific energies are associated with the Rider-Waite-Smith (RWS) cards we can take that information and apply it to further learning and application, including to other decks. Although imagery can vary from deck to deck, it is generally acknowledged that the energies and symbolism of the RWS deck hold true. So, although a deck you have in your house may not mirror the traditional RWS exactly— even the imagery in this book may not mirror the RWS imagery exactly—the symbolism is what is important.

A NOTE ABOUT THE DECK
You will notice throughout the book that card aspects, such as symbolism and color, do not always correspond with the presented illustration of the card. This is because, for those discussions, I reference the Rider-Waite-Smith (RWS) tarot deck. Rider-Waite-Smith is the classic deck that every novice begins with and every experienced practitioner returns to time and again to deepen their understanding of the cards. It is in this cycle of study and reinterpretation that tarot becomes a living medium. Because tarot endures, it evolves. I think the beautiful images in this book created by Stasia Burrington capture that perfectly.

Once we have a solid understanding of why each card holds its traditional energies, we can apply those energies to areas outside of divination, such as manifestation. The cards are loaded with symbolism that can be reflected in other areas of one's spiritual practice, even on a mundane level of manifesting the energy of that card for your daily life.

WHAT IS MANIFESTATION?

In this book, we will explore the basic energies associated with each of the Major Arcana cards so that they can be applied to your manifestation rituals, as well as to your practical rituals, charms, and spellwork.

What is manifestation? At the most basic, it is something's form or the form that it takes. It is a tool I have used to bring forth the energies or events I want in my life, through witchcraft and magick. Although there are other ways to manifest—not all people who use manifestation would consider themselves witches—this book uses ritual and spell-casting as tools for manifestation.

The tools used for manifestation ritual work can vary from practitioner to practitioner, but they often include the Major Arcana due to its heavy use of symbolism. That symbolism is an easily accessible tool for manifestation work. Why not use it for the energies or events you want to call forth in your life?

My hope is that this book pushes you to think outside the box in magick and witchcraft. Not everyone can pour money into their craft when they are first getting started, but luckily, we all have access to the imagery of the RWS tarot, even if simply in a printed image. Thinking creatively can push us as magickal practitioners, now and in the future.

2

BUILDING A RELATIONSHIP WITH YOUR CARDS

You will continue to grow and learn how to build your relationship with tarot throughout your life. Although a basic understanding of the cards is important when you begin, new meanings and correspondences will become clear to you over time. In the beginning, you should base connecting with your deck around connecting with the symbolism and energy of each card. If you have just purchased your first deck, you may find yourself anxious to open the box and dive right into a reading without much understanding of the cards. As appealing as that may be—and although I am not opposed to this—I do implore you to follow some of these tips to building your relationship with your deck. This will not only lead to a better intuitive process, but will also open the doors to your using the cards magickally.

BONDING WITH YOUR DECK

Tarot is full of esoteric, numerological, astrological, and biblical symbolism. When we understand the energies associated with the cards via their symbolism, we can apply that knowledge to other magickal uses. For example, we can use tarot cards as a numerological placeholder or to represent two people, thanks to their zodiac associations. Once you understand the foundational *why*, you open the doors to never-ending possibilities.

Before doing anything, it's always good practice to cleanse your deck! You can do this in whatever way is already natural to your growing practice. I prefer suffumigation. Suffumigation is the act of cleansing with smoke—not to be confused with smudging, a sacred Native American practice. We do this by allowing smoke to cover our deck completely. It may take several minutes for the smoke to cover all the cards. Cleansing is not a race, so take your time. You can also cleanse your deck by placing a piece of selenite atop it for a few hours. Or you can place it in a bowl of salt or cleanse it using the sunlight. The list goes on and on—do what feels right for you.

Many witches and practitioners recommend sleeping with your deck as you build a bond with it. This practice is not required, and any superstition that tells you otherwise is just that: a superstition. However, it is an intimate way to speed up your bonding experience with your cards.

When you first build a bond with a deck, I recommend that you shuffle with your left hand. Down the line this isn't something one *needs* to do, but the left represents the subconscious, and this simple act connects us to that deeper plane of intuition and subconscious feeling. Again, this is not a requirement, but it is my recommended practice when you are learning a new deck.

Ask questions you know the answers to already to see how your deck responds. Some decks are harsher, while some meet you with a velvet glove. Find out how direct your deck is for future interpretation. Getting to know how your deck answers your questions will make ritual work easier as well. If you have a harsh deck, you may find it less flexible as a ritual tool.

LEARNING THE CARDS

My first tip for any form of learning is to take your time. Tarot is a practice, something that we never stop learning. You don't need to have it down in a day so you can start charging people. If that is your intention, well . . . maybe tarot isn't for you.

Start by learning one card or one grouping of cards at a time. Maybe start with just the Major Arcana or a suit in the minors. Maybe start with just learning the five cards associated with the number eight. Or maybe just start with the one. Remember, it's not a race. Sit with this focus for at least a week. If you are keeping a grimoire for tarot, take note of the symbolism, numerology, colors, and esoteric icons.

Start with the basic Rider-Waite-Smith interpretations before branching out to your meanings. This isn't to suggest you should ignore your intuition—jot your thoughts down in your grimoire as they come to you and revisit them when focusing on spreads or daily pulls. If the themes continue to crop up, that is your intuition at play. Making note of it is important to your overall growth.

My biggest recommendation for learning about your deck is to keep a journal (in addition to your grimoire). Whether you are learning card by card or doing daily draws, writing down your readings/cards will develop your intuition and act as a great memory tool for learning each card, especially in the beginning. Our daily journal prompt should be open—no spreads or structured meanings, but simple questions such as:

What can I take from this day?
What are today's strengths?
What are today's weaknesses?
What advice should I take for this day?
What is something I need to let go of today?

When we pull a single or even partnered card with one of these simple prompts, we are focusing on the symbolism, the meaning, and our intuition. What do you feel when you see this card? What is your energy? What do you see within the card, and what does that mean? How would you apply this feeling and knowledge to your interpretation for the day ahead?

We can then revisit what happened during the day on the next morning before our next single pull. How did the day's events relate to the card you drew? Doing this will not only help you learn tarot; it will also build your intuition to a point where journaling is not necessary—though of course you can still journal if it helps your process.

3

APPLYING THE MAJOR ARCANA TO SPELLWORK

The only limit to the way you work your tarot cards into your magickal practice is your imagination. We can use tarot for divination to support our spellwork in a variety of ways, such as:

1. Foreseeing the outcome of a spell.
2. Gauging a timeline for the outcome of a spell.
3. Gaining foresight on any red flags or unforeseen consequences.
4. Receiving guidance on the kind of spellwork to perform.
5. Getting advice on practical follow-through after our spellwork.
6. Interpreting our dreams.

Outside of divination, tarot has myriad uses in our spellwork. You can use the cards:

1. As elemental or other markers, including those in this chart.

ELEMENT	SUIT	CARDINAL DIRECTION
Air	Swords	East
Water	Cups	West
Earth	Pentacles	North
Fire	Wands	South
Spirit	Majors	None, Self

2. On the altar to represent a goal or intention you are working on manifesting.
3. To release what no longer serves you.
4. As an energy focus for a meditation, using only a single card.
5. To channel a card, intentionally, through prophetic dreams, to see what your guides have to speak on regarding its energy.
6. As a representation of specific deities, gods, goddesses, spirits, and the like. This is not something I have covered in this book as it is in-depth and expansive enough to require a whole different book. However, I encourage you to research the connections and use them as easily accessible tools!

We can utilize the Major Arcana's symbolism and imagery as a powerful manifestation tool. The simplest way to do this is to use tarot in mental witchery to create positive affirmations and set goals. Although witchcraft is not a synonym for self-help, the two can correlate. We manifest the ideas and energies we are trying to bring to life through energy focus, spellwork, and/or prayer. Whether we choose to channel the energies associated with the card or use the power of our imaginations to focus on the symbolism of the card as it applies to our own life, a tarot card can be a powerful ritual tool.

Many tarot spells include crystals, candles, herbs, and/or oils in addition to tarot cards as the focal point of the spell. It is not necessary to include other aspects in your spell, however. Just as in any form of spellwork, you can always use substitutions; our intention is the most important tool we have available to us. The tarot card is sometimes placed underneath, behind, in front of, or to the side of a candle or crystal the spell requires. We are channeling the energy of this card, so its placement is in itself an element of this spellworking. Spellwork that has a tarot card as a primary focus often calls for the card to be left within view on one's altar for a certain duration. In some cases, you might also carry it on your person for a time or place it in a significant location that correlates to the spellwork.

Although the Major Arcana is the arcana primarily used in spellwork and is our focus for this book, this isn't to say that the minors are excluded. The majors' focus is on karmic influences and the big archetypal themes that are influencing your life. Therefore, majors are the easiest to translate into ritual and spellwork. But if you are using a minor suit, or card(s) feel more appropriate to you, by all means, do not feel as though you are held back.

4

THE MAJOR ARCANA

00 THE FOOL

ZODIAC	Aquarius
RULES	Uranus
ELEMENT	Air
COLOR	Pale yellow
AS A YES OR NO QUESTION	Yes
UPRIGHT	Beginnings, free spirit, innocence, spontaneity, starting over, freshness, brightness, youth, extremes, beginning without end, infinite potential, optimism, freedom
REVERSED	Holding back, restlessness, risk-taking, foolish behavior, mental disorders, recklessness, instability, childlikeness, naiveté, dangerous foolishness

The Fool's journey is the overarching theme of the Major Arcana. The Fool is the bright beginning, and the following twenty-one cards are his story.

The Fool is depicted with his back turned to the warmth of the sun, embracing the sun's yellow sky. Not all is revealed to him just yet. Despite this air of unknowing, The Fool still holds enthusiasm, optimism, and a childlike sense of wonder. The sun shines from the right-hand corner of the card, reminiscent of a sunrise. Its placement, if you take into account esoteric teachings, represents the sun that never sets.

00 THE FOOL

THE FOOL'S SYMBOLISM

The Fool holds a white rose, which represents purity and innocence. He himself is a bit innocent and naive, but not in a negative way. Much like a child, he is unafraid of the future. Although we may consider his blind optimism illogical by today's standards, it allows him to open up endless possibilities. The world is his oyster. The same is said about the dog, which is also white in the original RWS deck. Left to nature, the dog is a wolf, but human intervention domesticates it. The white dog is also a representation of intellect, a human condition that is lower than the spiritual cosmic egg from which we spring.

In the RWS version, The Fool holds a red knapsack and has red brimming around his sleeves. This knapsack contains all his hidden desires and hopes for his future as well as his essential needs. Red is a primary color and is generally associated with action and power. The red knapsack is tied to a wand, the essence of actions. The pouch, which represents the subconscious, is full of his past memories. He has not utilized the past lives in his pouch consciously, but he is ready to learn how. The red feather in his hat is a symbolic representation of his desire, passion, and truth.

The mountain peaks in the background are cold and snow-covered, a reminder of the accomplishments awaiting each of us on our journey through life. They are contrasted against the foreground The Fool stands upon, which reminds us of the mathematical concept of fractals. Up close, the mountains in the RWS card look like a pile of rocks, but from a distance, they rise into beautiful, mathematical perfection.

The Fool is not even looking where he is going; he is so close to a cliff that he could fall at any moment. Again, we see The Fool symbolizing trust in the universe and the belief that we are headed in the right direction, thus the name *The Fool*. By all accounts, this mentality is foolish, but the universe provides him with safe passage even if he is not checking every angle of the path ahead.

THE FOOL IN MAGICKAL WORK

Energies: New projects, job applications, transitions, starting college, new chapters of our life, moving somewhere new, adventures, safe travels, fertility

Lunar Phases: New moon, full moon

The Fool is all about fresh starts and new beginnings approached with blind faith, as we have discussed. When using it as a symbol of manifestation, we look at themes of blind faith and dumb luck. Sometimes in life we must have hope that our paths will go in the direction we want them to take.

Hypothetically speaking, if you want to land a new job but haven't started the path of application yet, you would ideally use The Fool in spellwork that helps you to find a job that is right for your path.

You can also use The Fool in spellwork targeted at quelling or settling issues surrounding anxiety. The Fool isn't afraid of anything; he is fearless and dives in feet first. Although anxiety is a complicated matter that won't just go away with a simple ritual, you can work with or hone the energies of The Fool to help with anti-anxiety manifestation.

In rare instances, you can use The Fool for energies such as fertility. Although this would not be my go-to option for manifestation, their energies still align. After all, conceiving a child can only happen a few days per month. Having optimism that we will be successful in this limited window mirrors The Fool's energies. His childlike wonder can also directly symbolize the child you want to manifest.

Use this card paired with either the new moon or the full moon. The new moon is all about fresh starts, new projects, transitional periods, and much of the paralleled energies that match directly with The Fool. The full moon is when the moon is at its fullest and strongest potential. Although the symbolism may not match that of the new moon, it will give your spellwork for new beginnings that extra boost you may be looking for! Touching lightly to lunar phases, you can use The Fool as a symbol for the Maiden. If you work with the Triple Goddess, this beginning phase of The Fool aligns perfectly with her energy. Much like him, she is the beginning of one's life journey.

LANDING THE JOB

The Fool is all about fresh starts and new beginnings. What is a better example of beginning again than landing a new job or career you are hoping for? Although not all the correspondences below are required to make this a success, it is important to maintain at least one or two. Try to keep this spell as near to your interview date as possible.

Lunar Phases: New moon, waxing moon
Day of the Week: Sunday
Astrological Moon Phase: Moon in Taurus or Virgo

INGREDIENTS
- The Fool tarot card
- Job Incense (see below)
- Green or orange candle
- Tiger's eye or citrine
- Charcoal disk for burning loose or powdered incense
- Cauldron or thurible (for burning incense)

INSTRUCTIONS
Use The Fool card, representing the energy we are working with, as a place marker on your altar. You can either pre-make the loose incense or make it during your spell. If you have a mortar and pestle, powdering the incense is preferred. Engrave the candle with the name of the job you are focusing on getting. Light the incense on the charcoal disk, pass your crystal of choice through the smoke, and say the spell as follows:

> Like The Fool my success is guaranteed,
> To help me get the job I seek.
> Like The Fool my luck is assured,
> To help me earn the job I seek.
> The key to success is in this [name of stone]
> To help me acquire the job I seek.

After performing this spell, carry the stone with you to any job application or interview. Store excess incense for later use.

JOB INCENSE
- 1 part chamomile
- 1 part basil
- 1 part dragon's blood
- 1 part lucky hand

01 THE MAGICIAN

ZODIAC	Gemini and Virgo
RULES	Mercury
ELEMENT	Air
COLOR	Gold
AS A YES OR NO QUESTION	Yes
UPRIGHT	Ability, adaptability, applied knowledge, confidence, divine guidance, divine understanding, insight, magick, manifestation, mastery, occult, potential, preparedness, pure possibility, self, teacher and student, understanding
REVERSED	Conniving, ego, greed, illusions, lack of mental clarity, lack of preparation, manipulation, thief, trickery, untapped ability

The Magician represents the beginning of The Fool's journey. Rich with symbolism, a man stands before us in a white gown and red mantle. His double-layered robe represents his own spirituality and the power to make his dreams a reality. The white in his gown is a longstanding symbol of peace, clarity, illumination, innocence, and a divine kind of understanding. His red mantle brings the power, energy, and drive to make his desires possible.

01 THE MAGICIAN

THE MAGICIAN'S SYMBOLISM

In his right hand, The Magician holds a double-ended candle pointed toward the sky, toward the universe. He is drawing down powers from the universe in order to use them in the material world. The double-tipped white wand suggests a pure channel of one's spiritual wisdom and clear inspiration. The Magician's grip on the wand shows us his firm grasp of both intention and will.

On the table lie the physical tools he has available; all he needs to manifest whatever reality he desires is there. They include a sword, a pentacle, a cup, and a wand, the symbols on the suits of the Minor Arcana. These symbols are also found in traditional European occult magick, and they represent the four elements: Air, Earth, Water, and Fire, respectively. Their presence on this card shows us that not only is the divine on the side of The Magician—the universe is as well.

Above The Magician's head, we see an infinity symbol, also known as a lemniscate. A lemniscate in algebraic geometry is any eight-shaped figure. It has become a symbol of the infinite, also seen in other representations such as the snake eating its own tail. Its presence represents The Magician's ultimate and unlimited power of creativity. Willingly holding his active right arm upward and his left arm downward allows an open two-way channel of universal energy. This channel retains the pure potential for him to create and re-create whatever he wills in the earthly plane.

Finally, observing the garden surrounding The Magician, we see roses, lilies, and various flowers and leaves. This growth, this garden, shows us the abundance and potential The Magician has already manifested around him. Lilies are a symbol of purity, truth, and purpose while red roses, like those on the RWS card, mirror The Magician's mantle, bringing in the energy of power and passion. He already has growth surrounding him, and with all the tools at his fingertips, he will continue to manifest abundance.

THE MAGICIAN IN MAGICKAL WORK

Energies: Abundance, power, creativity, any magick needing full or extra strength

Lunar Phases: Full moon, waxing moon

Use The Magician in magick during the full moon or the waxing moon. The full moon, or esbats, is when the moon mirrors the energy of The Magician. It is at its fullest potential and has the highest lunar energy. We reserve esbats for magick that needs your highest energy pull, and The Magician is no different. The waxing moon draws energy in and can therefore be a useful correspondence with this card. That said, however, I would not pair The Magician with the waxing moon as a first pick, but it is a great alternative if you have missed the full moon.

The Magician brings us the energy of pure potential; he is a bit of a jack-of-all-trades. We use The Magician, much like the full moon, to hone energies that need our full energy and potential. He is the witch's card. Because this card is so open-ended, our focus is the use of the self, tapping into our power. We are looking at magickal energies that deal with you and manifesting potential in your own life. I would not use it when helping someone you know. You are the divine spark (for our purposes here), not those around you.

The Magician can be used in spellwork targeting major life shifts. The Magician mirrors the same energy as The Fool, who is about new beginnings, but focuses more toward self-starting. Unlike The Fool's dumb luck, The Magician is purposeful, driven, and holding a lot of calculated energy. Applying for a job that will launch your career? Consider magick surrounding this card. This is the kind of energy we are looking at.

As The Magician is all about the self and confidence, it is perfect to use in magick involving confidence and glamour magick. Use it as a tool when charming a necklace or ring to bring self-confidence. Or use it to bring yourself a voice before public speaking. Confidence is key, and The Magician's magick exudes this energy.

CARRYING YOURSELF WITH PRIDE

The Magician knows that he has all the tools to make his dreams a reality. We also often have the tool we need before us, but we lack the confidence to see it forward. Charming a small object to keep with us aids us in applying those tools with a brave and confident face. Whatever situation you've found yourself in, you've worked hard to get there, so help yourself with an added boost of confidence.

Lunar Phases: Full moon, waxing moon
Day of the Week: Friday
Astrological Moon Phase: Any fire sign moon

INGREDIENTS
- Laurel or black pepper essential oil
- Carrier oil
- The Magician tarot card
- Red candle
- Sage or dragon's blood incense
- Cauldron or thurible (for burning incense)
- Rose quartz, either a pocketable stone or in a piece of jewelry

INSTRUCTIONS
Before beginning, please make sure that your essential oil is in a carrier oil of some form to avoid harming your skin or the stone (especially if you opt for the hotter black pepper oil). The Magician should either be placed on your working altar or propped up with your ritual tools before beginning. Light the candle. Using the oil, anoint the rose quartz while repeating this charm three times:

I hold my head up high;
I have all the tools I need.
Make me happy;
I have all the tools I need.
I am filled with confidence;
I have all the tools I need.
I am my own Magician;
I have all the tools I need.

After performing your charm, let the incense and candle burn until they are eliminated. Wear or carry the rose quartz with you in all future situations that require a confidence boost. You may cleanse and recharge your rose quartz between encounters, under the appropriate moon (a full moon or a Monday or Friday waxing moon).

02 THE HIGH PRIESTESS

ZODIAC	Virgo
RULES	Moon
ELEMENT	Earth
COLOR	Light blue, silver
AS A YES OR NO QUESTION	Unclear. There is no straightforward answer; it is dependent on the querent's own intuition.
UPRIGHT	Akashic records, ancient knowledge, astral body, divine femininity, dreams, female dichotomy, introspection, intuition, knowing, meditation, Mother Goddess, secrets, stillness, subconscious mind, women's mysteries, the moon and stars, Triple Goddess
REVERSED	Addictions, disconnection from intuition, jealousy, manipulation, negative side of secrets, the other woman, withdrawal

The High Priestess is an ongoing tribute to intuition, female mysteries, and the stages of a woman's life. She is highly connected to Persephone and Hathor. There is a recurring theme that she, observing stoically, is all-knowing. Her intuition tells her the truth without allowing her expression to reveal her secrets; she has a divine poker face.

The number two plays heavily into The High Priestess's symbolism. It is a numerical representation of balance; The High Priestess's even-keeled, intuitive brain views situations with a balanced perspective.

02 THE HIGH PRIESTESS

THE HIGH PRIESTESS'S SYMBOLISM

We see a calm woman sitting between two pillars of white and black. Each has accents of the other's color, a direct connection to yin and yang. While sitting between these two pillars, she becomes a symbol of all-knowing; between two sides of every story, there is the truth. These pillars are a reference to the biblical pillars that stood on the porch of Solomon's Temple, the first temple in Jerusalem.

In The High Priestess's hand is a book, but we can only see a few letters—*Tora*—of the book's title. This book may be the ancient Torah, or the title may be the rearranged word *tarot*. She guards the book's secrets by not revealing the full title, but whether it is an allusion to the Torah or tarot, it is no doubt referring to her all-knowing nature.

Her crown and veil are further references to deep intuition and boundless knowledge. The moon is associated with women's mysteries and our divine feminine intuition. The High Priestess's crown is one of the ancient Celtic symbols for the cyclical nature of the female: Maiden, Mother, Crone. She has been through all stages of life, and she has the wisdom and insight to show for it. The moon at her feet also represents this, pairing with the Maiden stage of the lunar lifespan.

The wall of pomegranate behind The High Priestess is a reference to the Greek goddess Persephone and her husband Hades. This symbol is one of the underworld and the cycles of life. Much like the Celtic Triple Goddess, the garden portrays life, death, and rebirth. The pomegranates represent the female or feminine energies. It is a sign of union with the divine as well as union with others.

THE HIGH PRIESTESS IN MAGICKAL WORK

Energies: Intuition, truth, divination, otherworld, astral projection

Lunar Phases: New moon, dark moon, full moon

As she has a recurring theme of the Triple Goddess and magick that involves all stages of the moon, The High Priestess is suitable to use at any of the three-stage markers. If we are working with Maiden magick, we begin at the new moon, moving toward the dark moon for the Crone.

Although she is a card in the tarot deck, The High Priestess's all-knowing energies make her a perfect tool for divinatory rituals outside of tarot. After all, one is not limited to using tarot exclusively for divinatory practices. Before practicing a guided meditation, use her in spellwork to help connect with astral guides. The High Priestess also pairs perfectly with spellwork to call forth prophetic dreams. She is a card of intuition and truth, dealing heavily with the otherworld and nighttime. Focus on the all-knowing and that divine poker face. Focus on magick that reveals to you what you already know but have chosen to ignore. The subconscious holds many secrets, and to gain access we need only tap into it.

Astral projection is a tricky form of magick that very few have mastered, but if you are working with magick to help separate your physical body to the astral plane, you can use The High Priestess as a symbol of astral travel in preparatory spellwork.

DIVINATION DREAMS

Prophetic dreams are a common form of divination, and people often keep dream journals by their bedside table to record the night's dreamscapes. As witches, we may use our dream journal to push the dream further and understand their hidden messages. There are several possible spells to aid in this journey, but the one I find most helpful is a spell bottle. It's easy, and you can use it as long as you wish to maintain it.

Lunar Phases: Full moon, waxing moon
Day of the Week: Monday
Astrological Moon Phase: Pisces or Cancer full moon

INGREDIENTS

- Purple and/or silver candle
- The High Priestess tarot card
- Your preference of smoke for cleansing your spell bottle
- Bottle with lid
- Calendula
- Rose
- Mugwort
- Bay leaf
- Lemon peel
- Small enough moonstone or labradorite stone or chips (optional)

INSTRUCTIONS

To begin, light the candle(s), place The High Priestess card in plain sight on your working space, and light the cleansing smoke. Focus on cleansing your spell bottle. Clear the negative energy from your workspace. Layer calendula, rose, mugwort, bay leaf, lemon peel, and moonstone or labradorite into your jar one at a time.

Use candle wax to seal the jar. You can either:

- put a drop of wax on the lid and use it to adhere the candle to the lid, leaving it until the flame is exhausted, or
- drip the candle wax over the jar, until its lid is fully coated.

If you adhere your candle to the top of your jar, perform the following chant while it burns. Otherwise, hold your jar and chant your spell when the waxing stage is completed, leaving the remaining candle burning.

Moonlight, gone for the night.
High Priestess,
Send your power for my divination tonight.
High Priestess,
Give me dreams of future insight.

Your spell bottle should be placed near your bed or on your nightstand. Charge it regularly by moonlight, repeating the same chant every time.

Optional: Charge the jar any way you prefer. Try surrounding it with corresponding crystals. Leave it in the moonlight on the day and/or moon phases above. Keeping your spell bottle "topped off" will maintain its intentional energy.

03 THE EMPRESS

ZODIAC	Taurus and Libra
RULES	Venus
ELEMENT	Air
COLOR	Green
AS A YES OR NO QUESTION	Yes
UPRIGHT	Abundance, babies, beauty, birth, bounty, caring, femininity, fertility, loving, mother, motherhood, nurture, peace, pleasure, plenty, pregnancy, receptivity, unconditional love, warmth
REVERSED	Codependency, creative block, fertility problems, lack of abundance, smothering, unexpected pregnancy or problem pregnancy

The Empress is the mother and the feminine half of her partnership with The Emperor. Her full figure leaves us with the impression that she is either with child or that she recently had a child. Her clothing is loose and flowing, suggesting she is ripe with pregnancy. However, it is just a suggestion, which allows the observer to see the perceived pregnancy as both literal and figurative. The Empress's ability to nurture life is not limited to childbearing, as she is surrounded by grains and gardens. She breathes life and creativity into everything she touches.

03 THE EMPRESS

THE EMPRESS'S SYMBOLISM

In the RWS tarot deck, The Empress sits in front of a yellow background. Yellow is the color of energy, creation, and vitality. It represents the radiant, vibrant energy that brings forth all life. Without the sun, nothing on Earth can grow. It is a nourishing aspect of consciousness that The Empress uses to create, heal, and grow all her plants, her children, and everything else under the sun and stars. The green color of her vegetation in the original card is a product of the sun. She is the mother of all things.

Her crown of twelve stars and myrtle is sacred to the zodiac and to the goddess Venus, the Roman goddess of fertility and love. Venus is a recurring theme in this card, and her symbol, the mirror glyph, lies at The Empress's feet. In the RWS card, The Empress also wears pearls around her neck. Pearls symbolize purity, beauty, and spiritual wisdom, and they are sacred to Venus, who was born of the sea and is often depicted standing nude in an oyster or clamshell.

The Empress holds a scepter with a sphere resting on top. The scepter is a phallic symbol, representing male fertility, while the sphere represents the feminine. This symbol signifies the union of masculine and feminine aspects to bring about a period of creation. There are twelve zodiac signs and twelve months of the year. This signals that she is the great mother to everyone, as she encompasses the entire zodiac.

The trees surrounding The Empress are evergreen and cypress trees; cypress trees are related to Venus, and evergreen trees show us that even in the dead of Winter, we are still alive with new ideas and creative imagination. It doesn't matter what your situation is: There is always hope for breathing new life into it!

THE EMPRESS IN MAGICKAL WORK

Energies: Fertility, creativity, new projects, growth

Lunar Phases: Waxing moon, new moon

As The Empress is all about breathing new life into existence, she is the perfect tool to use for growth. This can be literal, such as fertility magick and aiding the conception of a baby, or more figurative, such as creative workflow. Or maybe you are trying to open a business or take a new step in your career. As The Empress is all about nurturing new projects and new life, wherever your personal garden needs tending, she's your girl.

The Empress is creative and passionate, and although we can use her to focus on literal birth matters, we also give birth to new ideas every day. She breathes more life into our day-to-day activities, such as artwork and free-flow thinking. If we are starting new projects that need that divine spark, she would be the ideal candidate to turn to. We are looking for her to nurture that creativity.

The Empress is the ultimate symbol of femme, which makes her a staple for all rituals that involve the need to hone our feminine energy. This can span from anything stereotypical, such as sensuality and intuition, to gender-related issues. Matters of the patriarchy and even gender identity can come into play when we are looking at traditionally feminine energies.

Use this card as a ritual tool during the lunar phases of the waxing or new moon. As the waxing moon helps us expand and grow in any form of magick we are working with, it pairs perfectly with the nurturing Empress. Meanwhile, the new moon is all about new beginnings and fresh starts. Use The Empress to start a new chapter with a positive mental attitude and the confidence to breathe life into any project you put your hands on.

EGG CANDLE

Symbolism is used heavily in fertility spells, from gourd spells to citrus spells. We find that seeds and eggs make powerful symbolic tools for manifesting pregnancy. This spell is one of visualization as opposed to chants or incantations. Our heavily symbolic ritual requires patience, time, and the commitment to sit down and really see what it is you want. Before performing this spell, be sure you can dedicate a large portion of your time to it. This spell may take only five minutes for those of you with an easy ability to visualize, but it could also take a lot longer. There is no "correct" timeframe, so be patient with yourself.

Lunar Phases: Full moon, waxing moon
Day of the Week: Friday
Astrological Moon Phase: Full Cancer moon

INGREDIENTS
- Raw egg
- Candle wax and wick (e.g., warm up tealights to remove the wicks and pour the wax)
- Small seeds of your choice
- The Empress tarot card

INSTRUCTIONS
We will set our intentions before, during, and after this spell. Take some time to be clear with yourself about what those intentions are before beginning.

First, prepare the egg. Gently poke a hole in the large end with a pin. Then use scissors or a craft blade to carefully expand the opening. Empty the yolk into a bowl and set it aside to use however you see fit (no food waste!). Gently wash the inside of the egg. Using either a small cup or the egg carton, place the egg in an upright position. Gently pour the melted wax into the eggshell (if you are using tealights, gently warm the candle on a warmer to melt the wax without damaging your wick). Add the wick and let the wax cool almost completely. When the wax is almost solidified, add the seeds to the top of your wax.

With your new egg candle in hand, hold it up to The Empress card and close your eyes. Imagine the seeds growing into a tree. The tree blossoms, first with flowers and then with fruit. Light the candle and place it on your altar next to The Empress card until the candle burns out. Once the candle is extinguished, bury what is left of the egg candle under a seed-bearing tree.

04 THE EMPEROR

ZODIAC	Aries
RULES	The Sun
ELEMENT	Fire
COLOR	Red
AS A YES OR NO QUESTION	Yes
UPRIGHT	Ambition, authority, defender, establishment, even temper, father, fatherhood, idealist, leadership, management, order, patriarchy, reason, regulation, stability, structure, truth, wisdom, working mentality
REVERSED	Bad father, bully, combativeness, cruelty, dictator, egocentricism, explosiveness, ruthlessness, temper, tyrant

The Emperor is the perfect equal of The Empress. He matches her divine femininity and softness with his divine masculinity, countering her softness with passion, leadership, and authority. These are, of course, stereotypical archetypes. The Emperor needs his Empress, for without her he becomes cold and his logic turns tyrannical. The love of his Empress is what gives him the strength of compassion. Without her soft touch, The Emperor's authority and structure hold no weight.

04 THE EMPEROR

THE EMPEROR'S SYMBOLISM

The Emperor is depicted as an older man with a white beard sitting on a throne. The Emperor's age, depicted by his white beard, shows us his wisdom. His gaze off to the right implies that he is looking to the future, always thinking of the next move before his potential enemies. He wears a crown symbolizing not only his leadership in the Major Arcana hierarchy but also his union to The Empress. Unlike with his counterpart, there is no lounging in this image. Instead, he is rigid and authoritative in stature. He sits, but he is ready for action at any moment.

Four ram heads form the four corners. The ram is a symbol of Aries, representing leadership, courage, and aggression. Ares is the Greek god of war, and The Emperor reflects this tone of commander in chief. He is suited in full armor and adorned with a red cloak. As red is the color of war and power, the cloak further pushes this energy of a leader with tough decisions to make. Like any commander in chief, The Emperor does not make decisions involving war lightly. He is calculated and cunning.

The narrow stream in the background again connects The Emperor to the divine feminine. Balance is important between these two cards. Furthering the balance between The Emperor and his Empress, he holds an orb and scepter, just as she does. This symbolizes the balance between the feminine and masculine energies; they need each other to function as a whole. Gender is a spectrum that craves balance. We are not wholly one or the other, but balanced.

THE EMPEROR IN MAGICKAL WORK

Energies: Authority, structure, power, passion

Lunar Phase: Full moon

When we work with The Emperor, we use the energy of power, authority, and dominance. Therefore, we will always use the most powerful lunar phases, such as a full moon, super moon, or blue moon. (In a rare instance, one could argue that the black moon can be used for extra power in hexes, curses, or the like. However, we do not discuss that form of magick in this book.)

Power can take many different forms, and one of the most recognizable is in the hierarchy of one's workplace. You may find yourself seeking a promotion, and with this comes stepping up your power in your workplace. You may also encounter other forms of asserting power, such as gaining leadership roles that do not come with a promotion but set you up for a leg ahead later.

Another time we see power coming into play magickally is taking control of one's power, which has become a popular form of fighting the patriarchy in recent years. This can range from anything involving self-confidence to learning to find your voice. In fact, many people beginning their witchcraft journey find themselves drawn to the craft as a form of taking back their power.

The Emperor is a perfect card to use with any kind of magick that deals with taking back power or control of a situation in which you are directly involved. Sometimes, we all need an extra boost to raise our vibrations and our tone, and to give us the confidence to stand up for what we are hoping to achieve.

FINDING YOUR VOICE

For this spell, focus on carrying yourself with pride and confidence. Remember that getting the job or promotion comes down to knowing you've already got it before you interview—without coming off as cocky, of course. There is a difference between cockiness and confidence, though, so find your balance. Using the authority of The Emperor, you can hone that energy and get the promotion you are seeking!

Lunar Phase: Full moon
Day of the Week: Sunday
Astrological Moon Phase: Full moon in Virgo

INGREDIENTS
- The Emperor tarot card
- Orange string
- Silver string or ribbon
- Green string or ribbon

INSTRUCTIONS
Place The Emperor before you along with the strings ready for braiding. Braid the three strings together, making it long enough to be worn as a bracelet during your promotional interview, job placement, or the like. While braiding the strings, repeat the following spell aloud:

On this Sunday night, I weave this spell
Of prosperity, success, and authority.
I ask all the positive energies in the Universe to bless me
*   with prosperity.*
I embody the energies that allow me to carry myself as The Emperor.
I weave this spell
Of prosperity, success, and authority.
I ask for aid in finding my voice to assert my power.
Everyone I meet looks to me with knowledge of power.
Everyone I meet looks to me with acceptance of stability.
So mote it be.

Wear the bracelet until you are promoted or given the higher job that you were seeking. Remember it is important to do the legwork, and then this woven bracelet of three will help secure your seat in promotions.

05 THE HIEROPHANT

ZODIAC	Taurus
RULES	Venus
ELEMENT	Earth
COLOR	Red-orange
AS A YES OR NO QUESTION	Unsure; no definite answer
UPRIGHT	Community, convention, doctrine, dogma, doing the right thing, learning, pope, religion, teaching, tradition
REVERSED	Abuse of power, bad mentors, breakdowns, going against the grain, poor guidance, rejection of community, unconventional methods or journey

The Hierophant is depicted wearing a red robe, suggesting his position of power within the community. The white accents that adorn his gown show us purity within his divine thought, implying that his spirituality and the higher voice he listens to are not tainted by his power or his position within his community. He is the ultimate symbol of religion, order, and spiritual messages between one and the universe. Spiritual leaders have always had a hand in projecting a community's power.

05 THE HIEROPHANT

THE HIEROPHANT'S SYMBOLISM

The Hierophant is reminiscent of a pope or a community's spiritual counselor. One of his hands points up to the sky, receiving God, and the other holds a golden staff with three crosses on it. The staff mimics the oversized crown that The Hierophant wears. Underneath his crown, we see he is wearing yokes that cover his ears. This suggests that his hearing does not come from human-to-human interaction. Instead, he is listening to the divine.

Unlike the two pillars we see on The High Priestess card, both pillars seen here are equal; there is no veil connecting the two. The High Priestess conceals her feminine knowledge behind her pillars' veil while The Hierophant has all his knowledge on display. There is nothing to hide; everything he has is sacred and free for all people to hear.

At The Hierophant's feet, we see two crossed keys and two monks kneeling before him. The crossed keys represent the merging of the feminine and masculine consciousnesses. Their knowledge is shared and equal. In the RWS deck, the monk on the left wears a gown of red roses while the monk on the right wears a gown of blue lilies. Red roses and lilies are symbols of the astral and physical worlds. Both monks kneel before The Hierophant just the same. The divine or astral plane has as much respect for him as the human or physical world. The two monks show their subservience to the teacher. Given the duality of the roses and the lilies, they can also represent two paths that a person can follow: a religious or spiritual path and a more academic path. Though, of course, academics are also simultaneously religious.

THE HIEROPHANT IN MAGICKAL WORK

Energies: Elder knowledge, community, ancestors, dogma, tradition
Lunar Phase: Any

The Hierophant is a tricky card when dealing with magick. Due to The Hierophant's association with dogma, community, elders, and tradition, it may be hard for some people to find a way to incorporate it into their spellwork. But even though witchcraft may not directly correlate to our conventional ideas of dogma, people from all walks of life have elders. We often seek out higher learning through those around us and the people in our lives who have learned by doing so that we don't have to repeat their mistakes.

The Hierophant is one of the few cards that we can use magickally with all lunar phases. When using this card, we are most often going to be drawing in information and learning from our ancestors and guides. Therefore, select a lunar phase based on the information you are seeking. (See page 140 for more on lunar phases.)

We may find ourselves meditating with The Hierophant card to gain deeper insight. As the card itself is a figure who hears messages from the divine, combining it with our meditations can symbolize the messages we seek from our guides.

Not all rituals need to follow a grand manifestation format. Sometimes a ritual is as simple as repeating something in a specific way. Knowing this, we can apply The Hierophant to our daily life rituals, from brushing our teeth to morning meditation. Once we establish the card within these rituals, we can consider a ritual in our daily life and observe what about it needs improvement or adjusting.

VOICES FROM DREAMLAND

Unlike the prophetic dream spell we saw with The High Priestess, The Hierophant helps us look at dreams with a message. We can apply this in meditation, too. We are simply listening to guidance for the present instead of looking forward. The Hierophant knows all, and therefore, we can take the opportunity to learn from the universe, our spirit guides, and so on, on how best to grow in the now.

Lunar Phase: Any
Day of the Week: Monday
Astrological Moon Phase: Full moon in Pisces

INGREDIENTS
- Mugwort-based tea*
- Glass of water
- The Hierophant tarot card
- Journal and pen (optional)

INSTRUCTIONS
Similar to The Empress card's spell, this spell is all about intention and waiting. About thirty to forty-five minutes before going to bed for the night, or before a long meditation, drink the mugwort tea. Mugwort has a long-established role in opening us up for divination-based guidance, especially in dreamlike states. Place the glass of water on your bedside table. This is not for you, but it is an offering for your guides, spirits, ancestors, or whoever presents themselves to you for the night. Place The Hierophant card alongside the water. Before going to bed for the night, take a moment to sit with the intention of opening yourself up to the guidance you will receive that night. Think of The Hierophant and everything he stands for and take just a moment to meditate on that energy. Optionally, you can set a pen and paper next to your bedside to write down your messages in the morning.

Mugwort tea is an herbal supplement, and you should always talk with your doctor before consuming it. Pregnant women especially should consult their doctor before consuming anything mugwort-based.

06 THE LOVERS

ZODIAC	Gemini
RULES	Mercury
ELEMENT	Air
COLOR	Orange
AS A YES OR NO QUESTION	Definite yes
UPRIGHT	Agreements, arrangements, balance, business deals, carnal desire, choice, commitment, decisions, duality, fate, feminine and masculine balance, friendship, healing, love, relationships, soulmates
REVERSED	Cold, detachment, disharmony, divorce, imbalance, infidelity, relationship issues, relationships breaking apart, terminated contracts, too many partners

Before us we see two figures who mirror the biblical imagery of Adam and Eve: a male figure and a female figure, both nude. Although their energies are in opposition, they are on equal grounds as both figures are sky-clad. The imagery of balance repeats itself more than once in this card. The Tree of Knowledge stands behind the woman, the Tree of Life behind the man. Without knowledge there is no human life, and vice versa. They are two sides of the human experience. This duality is why this card is associated with the zodiac sign of Gemini.

06 THE LOVERS

THE LOVERS' SYMBOLISM

An angel (thought to be Raphael) looms over The Lovers, watching from the sky. In the RWS card, the angel wears a purple robe, which represents spirituality and royalty. The man looks toward the woman, and the woman looks toward the angel. That is, the man looks to the physical, and the woman looks to the spiritual. This symbolism plays on stereotypical archetypes of masculine and feminine energies. The man's desire is more carnal and passionate as he looks toward the woman. He doesn't even notice the angel, while the woman gazes up at the angel as if awaiting a spiritual message. She knows the truth about the man's carnal desire. This duality also brings balance; if both were looking to the same place, they would be ignoring a key element. The mountain between the couple seems to point upward toward the angel. This connects the three figures, forming a divine trinity.

The woman stands next to the Tree of Knowledge, the biblical representation of temptation. It is the reason the two were removed from the Garden of Eden. Meanwhile, the man standing next to the Tree of Life brings an air of passion, the tree's leaves shaped almost like small flames.

The choice element of this card comes into play as we observe both the man and the woman having a choice. These two must choose between their earthly desires and their spiritual ones. The blessing comes from making the right choice and finding the balance between the two. Ignoring either the spiritual or the primal is the wrong choice. With choice, we find balance, and vice versa.

THE LOVERS IN MAGICKAL WORK

Energies: Love, sexuality, passion, unions, contracts, deals
Lunar Phases: Waxing moon, full moon, new moon

When using The Lovers for magick, we can work with every moon phase except the waning moon. The Lovers card is about bringing two people together, and therefore, we are drawing in energies. The ideal lunar phase would be the waxing moon, as it pulls in the energies we want to work with. You can also use both the full moon and the new moon, depending on your intention. The new moon, as it is for fresh starts and new beginnings, would be ideal for an intimate bonding ceremony between two consenting parties or for spellwork that focuses on business contracts. Meanwhile, the full moon is good for all that extra energy; we consider it for any spell using The Lovers that requires extra strength.

As The Lovers card deals with unions, we can examine it a few different ways. First, there is the obvious connection of The Lovers in the card's symbolism as well as in life. Unions can be as bonding as marriage or commitment ceremonies or they can be as fleeting as a one-night stand. From whichever perspective you look at it, two people are coming together. When using The Lovers card in magick, we bring two people together, either for love or for more mundane reasons, such as contracts and business exchanges. This card would be perfect to draw in love around you by using it in a love spell. This would not be for a love spell to target a singular person but instead to draw in your soulmate. You can be specific about what you are looking for as long as you aren't keeping any one particular person in mind. Think about what you want from a mate and focus on that energy. The Lovers card is connected heavily to soulmates, so utilizing this energy for finding your own soulmate is simply logical.

ATTRACTING A SOULMATE

Attracting a soulmate is a journey and not one that happens instantly. You should release any notion you had of a simple light switch spell. The universe works on its own time. Be specific, without asking for a specific person, and allow the great wide universe to do her magick.

Lunar Phase: Waxing moon
Day of the Week: Friday
Astrological Moon Phase: Moon in Virgo

INGREDIENTS

- The Lovers tarot card
- Pink candle
- Red candle
- Gold candle
- White candle
- Cauldron
- Pen
- Several bay leaves

INSTRUCTIONS

Focus on the setup of this spell. Place The Lovers card in the center of your altar with two candles on each side. (Be sure to leave some space to avoid a fire hazard.) In front of this setup, arrange the cauldron in a place that is fire safe; please be careful and be mindful of where you perform this spell.

On the bay leaves, write down all the things you look for in a partner. Remember not to write down a name or think of someone specific. We are talking about emotional connections here. Then, burn our bay leaves in the cauldron while saying this spell:

With bonding example that is The Lovers
By Earth, Air, Fire, Sea
Please draw love to me.
Someone who is connected to my soul,
Once together, we shall be whole.
I give love freely,
I will accept love completely.
Find me this Lover,
Draw them to me.
As I say, so shall it be.

Allow the candles to burn out. Collect the ashes from your cauldron. You can handle the ashes in one of two ways: Go to a river and hold the ashes for a moment, visualizing the spell and your requested partner, and then toss them into the stream. Or you can bury the ashes with a rosebush until you find your love.

07 THE CHARIOT

ZODIAC	Cancer
RULES	Moon
ELEMENT	Water
COLOR	Yellow
AS A YES OR NO QUESTION	Yes
UPRIGHT	Ambition, confidence, control, drive, movement, perseverance, protection, success, transportation, travel, tunnel vision, victory, willpower
REVERSED	Aggression, burn-out, car crash, ill thought-out action, lack of control, lack of direction, impulsivity, rushing, scattered energy, unhealthy obsession

The Chariot's driver seems to be steering two sphinxes to a finish line; however, if we look closely, no reigns are keeping the sphinxes in place. He uses his mind and mental capacity to control them. This reflects mastery over a situation and your own life. The sphinxes, one black and the other white, repeat the ongoing yin and yang imagery that we have seen in other cards leading up to this one. They bring symmetry and a balance that allows the driver to maintain equal control with ease.

07 THE CHARIOT

THE CHARIOT'S SYMBOLISM

The presence of the sphinxes on The Chariot card shows us its duality—both driven and emotional. We make the conscious choice to control our emotions when needed, to ride to victory.

Behind the sphinxes on the chariot cart front is a symbol that looks like a perfectly balanced spinning top, surrounded by wings. This symbolizes balance and mastery. If you are going to balance two opposing forces, such as the black and white sphinxes, you will need to be able to balance your mind, emotions, and body.

Going back to The Empress and The High Priestess, who both wear crowns with imagery of the night sky, The Chariot's driver wears a solar crown. The sun, compared to its lunar counterpart, has far more traditionally masculine energies. We are looking at the power, authority, and drive that the sun brings to us. If we look closely at the RWS version, however, we notice the moon is still present, seen on the driver's breastplates and suggested by a canopy of stars above him, while smaller stars surround the sun in his crown. His exterior is hard, like his zodiac's crab shell, but at his core he is still driven by the moon. Although his drive carries him to victory, this does not mean that he is free from the emotions of lunar correspondence.

The yellow skies in the background of the RWS card symbolize power and intellect. While the easily overlooked wand the driver holds in his right hand mirrors that energy, it's thought to be a physical director for his mental willpower and ability to control the sphinxes.

The function and ability for speech are associated with The Chariot. Our words matter. The things we say and think have a lot of power over how we live our everyday lives. The Chariot can drive to victory because before even leaving the gates, the driver knows he has total control of the situation. The same goes for how we speak to and about ourselves and our situations. Victory has many faces.

THE CHARIOT IN MAGICKAL WORK

Energies: Success, drive, passion, willpower
Lunar Phases: Waxing moon, full moon

When working with The Chariot in magick, focus on driving that "chariot" to success. When looking at this card strictly for magickal intent, think of it as having similar energy to The Emperor. We will always work with the waxing or full moon with The Chariot card. When our focus is on being successful in a given task, we are drawing in energy, not pushing it away. Therefore, the waxing moon is ideal to draw in success; it also gives us a broader date range to use The Chariot in magick than the full moon.

The Chariot works best with magick that demands willpower. Consider energies that are comparable to winning a race. It takes determination and willpower to be successful. If you are about to compete in any form of competition, The Chariot would be the ideal partner to work with to assure yourself that victory. Therefore, we view its energy very similarly to the energy we see with The Emperor. Races and competitions take a wide variety of forms. This could present itself as running a marathon and wanting to take home gold or competing against many others for a job. It's all subjective and therefore a very flexible card, despite its linear, driven nature.

TAKING HOME GOLD

When it comes to driving the figurative chariot to the finish line, sometimes all it takes is a little luck to push you to success. This spell is perfect for any situation in which you need that extra push. This success spell is quite open-ended and can be used for anything from athletic competitions to a competitive workplace.

Lunar Phase: Full moon
Day of the Week: Tuesday
Astrological Moon Phase: Full moon in Aries

INGREDIENTS
- Red candle, any shape, large enough to mark your intentions on
- The Chariot tarot card
- Carving tool or pen
- Black cat or Van Van oil (optional)

INSTRUCTIONS
Before beginning, hold the candle in your hand before The Chariot card. Take a moment to close your eyes and visualize your goal. What does it look like? What does it mean to you? Spend a moment with this thought and intention.

After meditating on your intention, either carve your intentions into the candle or draw them on the candle's glass casing. If you have chosen to use the optional dressing oil, this would be the time you dress your candle with it.

Light your candle and take a moment to visualize yourself as The Chariot driver; the finish line is your end goal. Meditate on the visualization that you are driving yourself to victory. Allow your candle to burn out.

08 STRENGTH

ZODIAC	Leo
RULES	Sun
ELEMENT	Fire
COLOR	Yellow
AS A YES OR NO QUESTION	Yes
UPRIGHT	Belief in oneself, confidence, control of self-doubt, determination, mind over matter, overcoming of obstacles, patience, purity, strength, willpower, wisdom
REVERSED	Brute force, fear, flakiness, low energy, lust, overly emotional mindset, putting your head in the sand, self-doubt, spiraling out of control, unreliability, unresolved issues

Strength focuses on taming our "inner beast" and on having both the strength and the patience to do so. The woman is wearing white and gray, which represent purity and wisdom. She wears a garland crown of roses, which shows us her prominence over the lion, but it is also a symbol of her love and compassion. Red roses in tarot tend to represent the material world. The woman may be an authority figure in this card, but she is more like a mother than a ruler.

08 STRENGTH

STRENGTH'S SYMBOLISM

Strength looks larger than the land behind her and larger than the land she stands upon—she is larger than life. She is a powerful figure who can tame anyone with diplomacy, reason, and logic. Levitating above her head is an infinity sign, representing her mastery over her emotions. She has tamed hundreds of lions before the lion in the picture. It bows down before her while gently, affectionately licking her arm.

In the RWS tarot card, the sky is tinted yellow and consumes most of the background; this represents emotional intellect, clarity, energy, and optimism. Although the mountains in the background are distant, their presence represents the stability of this card—a stability that is known without being overbearing. Meanwhile, the grass that the woman stands on, which is green in the RWS version, mirrors that in a more material way and brings an air of abundance to the card. Although abundance can take many forms, it is most recognized in material wealth.

Lions represent carnal desire, passion, material power, and brute force. They are wild beasts that by all accounts cannot ever truly be tamed. In Strength, they can represent the passion and desire burning inside a person. This passion and desire can be used both destructively and constructively, given the right instruments. The woman is using her spiritually divine nature to telepathically talk to and subdue the beast. We can decide how we want to use the lion's passion once it is subdued.

STRENGTH IN MAGICKAL WORK

Energies: Anger management, control, relaxation, peace

Lunar Phases: Waning moon, dark moon

When working with Strength, we are often trying to remove negativity—including poor attitudes—or we need a moment to relax. We work with the waning moon or the dark moon with this card, harnessing the waning moon to push away energies that no longer serve us and the dark moon to intensify this power. Much like the dark moon's counterpart, the full moon, it is reserved for more forceful pushing, as it is at its highest form.

Strength becomes useful in situations of high stress and when one needs to remain calm despite one's environment. Of course, this card is not great for most emergency situations, as we cannot usually pause them to say, "Excuse me, I need to do a ritual during this emergency." We can use it to prepare for stressful situations, however, such as a particularly high-stress workweek or toxic family dinner party. If we know the situation will test our patience, we can arm ourselves beforehand with a ritual to help us keep our cool and maintain our poise.

We can also use Strength for mindful meditation. Although meditation is not a ritual used to prevent stress, the Strength card can be a tool for aiding in peace and relaxation while you are meditating. Just as some people meditate with a crystal, you can place the Strength card with you, with purpose and intention, before beginning your meditation. There is patience in Strength, the same patience you must find within yourself when venturing into a meditation practice.

LETTING GO OF ANGER

Sometimes all we need to let go of a grudge or pent-up anger is a simple spell to release ourselves from those feelings. Anger and distaste are often feelings that are hard to shake. Release spells are the first step to letting go. Then you must follow them up with action. But sometimes all we need to run a full marathon is a gentle nudge toward the first step.

Lunar Phase: Waning moon
Day of the Week: Sunday
Astrological Moon Phase: Moon in Aquarius

INGREDIENTS
- Paper
- Pen
- The Strength tarot card
- White candle
- Matches or a lighter
- Cauldron or fire-safe bowl

INSTRUCTIONS
Sit down with the pen, paper, and Strength card and write down everything that has been causing you emotional grief. This could include anger toward a situation or a grudge against a person. If several things have been causing you grief, write them down on separate pieces of paper.

Light the candle. You will use it to burn the papers that hold the energies you intend to release. One by one, light each piece of paper with the candle flame and place it into the cauldron while repeating the following spell:

Strength, a card of patience,
I ask you to lend me your energies tonight.
In this darkness, my thoughts see no light.
Assist me in banishing this negativity,
And help me replace it with a calm mind.
I tame my lion
And release this energy.

When the spell is complete, clean up the ashes and dispose of them away from your home. This is an important symbol of letting go. Please do not litter. If you have burned your paper to ash, it should be safely disposed of in dirt, at least a mile from your home. You are no longer holding onto this energy, so you should also release the ashes that remain.

09 THE HERMIT

ZODIAC	Virgo
RULES	Mercury
ELEMENT	Earth
COLOR	Yellow-green
AS A YES OR NO QUESTION	Yes
UPRIGHT	A walk at night, analytical skills, astrophysicist, depth, humanitarian, inner guidance, insight, introspection, master, peace and quiet, prophet, retreat, sage, scientist, seeker of knowledge and esoteric knowledge, self-awareness, solitude, spiritual completion, thoughtfulness, wisdom, wise sage
REVERSED	Depression, isolation, lack of foresight, loneliness, not learning, repeating mistakes, self-doubt, self-pity, withdrawal

The Hermit holds a lantern with a star on it. We can interpret this star, a hexagram, either as the Star of David or the Thelma Unicursal Hexagram, both symbols of spiritual and philosophical viewpoints. From whichever viewpoint you see this hexagram, it shows that the universe guides The Hermit on his way and provides for him. To reach the heavens, all he must do is look before him. Another viewpoint is that the star is simply a beginning; we are all part of the universe and come from the stars.

09 THE HERMIT

THE HERMIT'S SYMBOLISM

The Hermit is a very introspective card. He is the tarot equivalent of turning off all technology and focusing inward without all the modern chatter. In the RWS card, we see an old man in a gray cloak holding up a lantern. He walks with a tall walking stick, or, more appropriately, a staff. Commonly associated with pilgrims and saints, the staff is often seen as an emblem of power and authority. The Hermit holds his staff in his left hand, symbolizing his higher awareness. His beard is white and long, implying his age and the wisdom that comes with it. His beard's unkempt state suggests that he is beyond caring about his appearance; his focus is only on his quest for wisdom. The material world and the beauty that comes with it do not appeal to him.

Behind The Hermit, the landscape is barren because he is focusing on only the light. Our Hermit is on a spiritual quest. In the original RWS version, the background is a darker blue, which fades into white. Dark blue symbolizes communication and enlightenment, especially when blending toward white.

If we look closely, we can see that The Hermit stands upon the precipice of an icy mountain. As he has reached the top of this mountain on his spiritual quest, we are looking at the energies of achievement, growth, and accomplishment. Although he has reached the top of this peak, he still finds himself searching further. This is a chosen path, not one of external pressure or demand. He has by all accounts reached his goal, yet he chooses to continue on.

THE HERMIT IN MAGICKAL WORK

Energies: Introspection, meditation, higher learning, spiritual guidance

Lunar Phases: Waxing moon, full moon

The Hermit card's use is less tangible than most cards. As this card focuses on learning and growth of mental and spiritual capacity, we won't necessarily be using it for a traditional spell or ritual work. Instead, I think of The Hermit similarly to how we view The Hanged Man: This is an Odin card. Odin's story of sacrifice for greater knowledge mirrors The Hermit's story. Although unlike The Hanged Man (page 80), there is no obvious sacrifice, there is still a real and subtle sacrifice occurring—the sacrifice of isolation. Because of The Hermit's isolating mental clarity and spiritual guidance, we are always drawing in with this card. We crave knowledge and ask for guidance. The Hermit will always use the lunar phases of the waxing moon or the full moon.

In spells or ritual workings, The Hermit's energies align well with guided meditations and divination, particularly scrying, automatic writing, and prophetic dreams. We are simply the vessel to receive the message, nothing more. We can place The Hermit as a marker of our intention before meditation or during divination, or we can specifically call out for guidance and use him as our guide.

There is intangible openness with The Hermit. Our intentions when using him should be simply to receive messages and guidance. This guidance should be without a specific intention; just be open to what you see and the messages presented to you.

STAR STUDENT

Test-taking is not just for high schoolers. Tests happen throughout our lives; after all, even the elderly have to take driving tests! Personally, test-taking is my biggest anxiety-inducing environment. I often completely blank on everything I have studied! This simple spell is a means of alleviating test-induced anxiety, ensuring that your hard work shines through. You put in the work—now watch it pay off.

Lunar Phases: Waxing moon, full moon
Day of the Week: Sunday
Astrological Moon Phase: Moon in Sagittarius

INGREDIENTS
- Citrine or pyrite
- Green mojo bag
- 1 part fern
- 1 part allspice
- 1 part dried cabbage
- 1 part cypress
- The Hermit tarot card

INSTRUCTIONS
Before beginning, make sure your crystal and bag are fully cleansed. This can be done via suffumigation, homemade sprays, solar cleansing, or salt cleansing.

Place all the herbs into a bowl or other container and mix them thoroughly. Transfer the fully combined herb mixture into the green mojo bag along with your crystal of choice.

Focus on visualizing with The Hermit. Place it before you, meditating on the symbolism of this card. While holding your mojo bag in hand, close your eyes and begin to picture a mountain. In this instance, you are The Hermit. Lantern in hand, you walk up your mountain, growing stronger, more knowledgeable, and more confident in time. Picture the mojo bag in your hands radiating a gold light, protecting you from outside influences and reinforcing the knowledge you already know.

After this ritual is complete, carry your mojo bag inside your bookbag, purse, or jacket pocket and take the bag with you to your test. You already have the knowledge. The mojo bag is simply there to ensure you can tap into it, shielded from external stress and anxiety.

10 THE WHEEL OF FORTUNE

ZODIAC	Sagittarius and Pisces
RULES	Jupiter
ELEMENT	Fire
COLOR	Violet
AS A YES OR NO QUESTION	Yes!
UPRIGHT	Call of destiny, change of destiny, cycles, cyclical progression, fate, gambling, good fortune, good luck, lottery, luck, movement, new beginnings, opportunity, positive karma, rewards, shift of energy, success, universal laws, up and down
REVERSED	Bad luck, downturn in fortune, lack of control, less luck, poor karma, rut

On the wheel in the center of this card, we can see the same four letters that adorn The High Priestess's book: T-A-R-O. The top symbol, which is below the letter "T," is Mercury. The second, which is beside the "A," is Sulphur. The symbol by the "R" is that of Water. The symbol across from the "O" is Salt. Between these letters, we see the symbols of the four elements in Hebrew. This furthers our understanding that this wheel is that of the all-encompassing universe; it is the higher knowledge of The High Priestess and the elements that make up all aspects of life.

10 THE WHEEL OF FORTUNE

THE WHEEL OF FORTUNE'S SYMBOLISM

The Wheel of Fortune is a busy card, and it is chock full of symbolism. In the center of the card is a wheel, which symbolizes the ever-changing wheel of life that supports our earth, universe, and life itself. Its orange color in the original RWS tarot card symbolizes the strength of the sun giving us life. In the center is another circle, which represents the exaltation of the moon.

The snake on the left of the wheel is an ancient symbol of rebirth, dating back to ancient Egypt and biblical lessons. In Christian theology, the snake persuades Eve to bite from the apple of knowledge; in a sense, she is reborn as a new, more insightful person. It is also thought that the snake is Typhoon, the deadliest creature in Greek mythology.

There is a jackal with a human body pressed against the lower right border of the wheel. This symbolism comes from the ancient Egyptian god Anubis, the god of mummification. In this sense, Typhoon represents bad luck, whereas Anubis represents good fortune and a rise to success. There is a balance between the two. Atop the wheel sits a sphinx with the sword of discernment. He is the great equalizer.

The bull, the lion, and the snake are all ancient symbols of rebirth. It's something like this: The sun eats the moon, but the moon is stronger, gets reborn, and eventually becomes full again. The lion, which represents the sun, eats the bull. That turns into the eagle and the sun eating the snake. This death and birth are companions in an infinite loop.

THE WHEEL OF FORTUNE IN MAGICKAL WORK

Energies: Luck, fortune, success, change of a life cycle, new beginning

Lunar Phases: New moon, waxing moon, full moon

The Wheel of Fortune is one of the luckiest cards to get in the Major Arcana for more than one reason. This is a card of success and good fortune. But it also represents the change of a life cycle, which opens the doors to whatever new chapter we want for ourselves. The obvious moon to partner with this card is always the new moon, as it signifies new beginnings. However, the luck and success that come with this card also open the doors for us to use the full moon and waxing moon. When performing magick such as luck spells or success spells, we are drawing in the energies we want to hold. Thus, the lunar phase we pair with The Wheel of Fortune depends on which kind of luck we are working with.

We partner The Wheel of Fortune with a few kinds of rituals, namely luck, success, and life cycle change. We can use this card when performing personal sabbath rituals that celebrate the change in the wheel of the year. In these cases, we use it simply as a symbolic marker of our acknowledgment in the season moving forward. When performing magick, we can call in its energy to bring us luck, such as before heading to a casino or something similar. And as we have seen with other cards leading up to this, such as The Magician and The Emperor, we can use The Wheel of Fortune for success in the workplace, such as spellwork for promotions or landing a job.

LUCKY HANDS

Gambling is all about luck. Now, I am not suggesting that you should do this spell and then spend your life savings on lottery tickets, but it's not a bad thing to push some energy in your favor before heading to a casino. This oil comes directly out of my book of shadows; I keep it for use with family, and it is a personal favorite of my gambling grandma. Create this ritual oil at your altar space and then take it into the casino with you. Keep luck at your fingertips when you roll the dice!

Lunar Phase: Waxing moon
Day of the Week: Thursday
Astrological Moon Phase: Any fire sign moon

INGREDIENTS
- The Wheel of Fortune tarot card
- Dropper or roller ball oil bottle (I prefer a dropper as it makes for quicker application and has more space)
- Ground cinnamon
- Elderberries
- Red clover
- Sweet almond oil
- Wintergreen essential oil
- Vanilla essential oil

INSTRUCTIONS
Before beginning, suffumigate the bottle to cleanse it.

Place the herbs into the bottle. I prefer to use seven pieces/parts per ingredient, as seven is a lucky number in numerology. Fill the container halfway with sweet almond oil, as a carrier. Add the essential oils; again, I prefer seven drops of each. Once the essential oils are combined, top off your bottle with sweet almond oil.

This bottle should sit to charge on either your altar or above or alongside your Wheel of Fortune card. You can also set your oil on a windowsill to let the herbs settle into the carrier oil for one week. Place a few drops of the oil on the palms of your hands before gambling. I personally prefer to top this up every few hours and keep this short chant in mind:

Everything I touch turns to gold,
Everything I want, I get threefold.

11 JUSTICE

ZODIAC	Libra
RULES	Saturn
ELEMENT	Water
COLOR	Green
AS A YES OR NO QUESTION	If the question is moral, yes; if otherwise, no.
UPRIGHT	Balance, cause and effect, courthouse, judges, justice, karma, laws, lawyers, marriage, scales of fate, trials
REVERSED	Bias, bigotry, delay in justice, dishonesty, getting ripped off, racial profiling, system working against you, unfair trial/court, unfairness

The woman on the Justice card looks like a judge. She is holding a sword so she can cut to the heart of any situation. The sword represents discrimination. She can easily look into a situation and see the truth. The gold scale she holds in her other hand balances her truth. She is the ultimate supreme court justice, being unbiased on a true and ethereal level. This card shows us an ethereal ability for balance, synthesis, and examining everything fairly.

11 JUSTICE

JUSTICE'S SYMBOLISM

In the original RWS Justice tarot card, a woman sits in front of a purple backdrop that is supported by two pillars. The backdrop represents her protecting the verdict. It also assures you that karmic retributions are working behind the scenes. You know they are there, but you can't see them. The original's yellow background behind the curtain connects Justice to the sun, which is an esoteric meaning you can delve much further into.

The two pillars represent duality. These pillars are the same pillars we see with The High Priestess, except the pillars on The High Priestess card are black and white. Both pillars on the RWS Justice card are gray (a mixture of The High Priestess's black and white) to represent synthesis and balance. You can take from what is above and synthesize from what is below.

JUSTICE IN MAGICKAL WORK

Energies: Justice, scales of fate, karma, legal proceedings

Lunar Phase: Any, depending on intention

Justice is one of the few cards that is truly open-ended regarding which lunar phase to work with, as depending on our intention, we could be pushing or pulling energy. Justice's usage, like its yes/no answer, depends on the situation. For example, if you are working with energies dealing with legal proceedings, you may be trying to avoid jail time. That would mean working with the waning or dark moon. If you are trying, however, to win a case involving a monetary reward, you would use the waxing or full moon, as these pair with the energy of attraction. If you are doing an "instant karma" spell, you can use Justice with the new moon, as you want to start a new chapter, with or without the target of the instant karma spell. That's why the lunar phase is so open-ended; we must examine what our intentions are before we can choose.

Magick that involves the Justice card will always deal with some form of the scales of fate, whether you want them to tip in your favor or someone else's. Think of justice being served or being bent in your favor. In most cases you can see this literally in court proceedings; perhaps it is magick that makes the judge sweet to you or opens the jury's eyes. If someone has hurt you in an intentional, malicious way, you may want to consider an instant karma spell—Justice would be a perfect partner for this!

SPEED UP KARMA

This spell is a bit of karmic retribution. This isn't something you do to harm someone intentionally or specifically. It is just a means of sending them back what they did to you and letting the universe decide what that punishment should be. Karma is typically seen as something that happens in the next life, not the present, so don't expect for their whole lives to be ruined. However, you can expect some of the energy they sent you to return to them.

Lunar Phase: Full moon
Day of the Week: Tuesday
Astrological Moon Phase: Full moon in Aries

INGREDIENTS

- The Justice tarot card
- Paper
- Pen
- Envelope
- Stamp
- 1 black candle
- Incense, preferably clove or cinnamon
- Cauldron or fire-safe bowl

INSTRUCTIONS

Doing a karmic retribution spell of this nature may be a more painful process than you realize. Please make sure you are in a safe headspace before going into this kind of spellwork.

The scales of justice are your main focus for this spell. Place the Justice card on your altar, channeling this energy for your intention. Take some time and write out a letter describing your pain, sorrow, and frustrations to your target. The letter should describe how their actions affected you. Be as descriptive as you see fit. Once you have written your letter in full, place it into the envelope, seal it, and stamp it. You don't need to write the person's address, but putting their name on the outside of the envelope, as if the letter were to be sent to them, is helpful.

Light the black candle. Use its flame to ignite the letter to your target and place the letter in the cauldron to burn safely. Allow the letter to burn completely, until it is ash, while saying the following:

The pain you have caused is no longer mine to own.
The hurt you have given, I send back to you.
Justice is here,
I am not alone.

After completing this spell, throw the ashes either into the wind or into a moving river. This will assure swift effect in your retribution.

12 THE HANGED MAN

ZODIAC	Pisces
RULES	Neptune
ELEMENT	Water
COLOR	Pale blue
AS A YES OR NO QUESTION	Very question dependent, but in most cases no
UPRIGHT	Faith, fate, fate in God's/the Universe's hands, letting go, martyr, new perspective, Odin, patience, pause, sacrifice, surrender, wisdom
REVERSED	Ego, impulsivity, missed opportunity, playing the victim, rash decisions, refusing to let go

The Hanged Man's hands are behind his back, possibly bound, possibly set in contemplation. His bound hands form a triangle shape behind him. Only one leg is tied to the tree branch while the other leg forms an inverted number four. Four, when upright, suggests completion, safety, and stability. When four is in reverse, however, we see someone who is waiting for spiritual wholeness but has not quite achieved it yet.

12 THE HANGED MAN

THE HANGED MAN'S SYMBOLISM

We see a man hanging upside down from a healthy Tau cross-shaped tree. Tau is the final letter of the Hebrew alphabet. *Tau cross* has many meanings; it is the symbol of the meeting place between the earth and the sky, bringing the deeper spiritual aspect of the card into play.

The red on the man's pants in the RWS tarot card denotes a passion for his beliefs. Think of The Hanged Man as you would think of Odin: He sacrifices himself for the passion, belief, and desire to hold power. You must have a will and passion to sacrifice yourself so boldly. We do not know how long the man will hang here (much like Odin) to get the knowledge he desires. Only time will tell.

The blue on The Hanged Man's shirt in the original is symbolic of water. Water reverses any image that reflects off its surface, and The Hanged Man's keyword is *reversal* because he reverses his thoughts and everything that he thinks he knows.

Around The Hanged Man's head is a shining light, reminiscent of the classic lightbulb cartoon that suggests a bright idea. The yellow light in the RWS version symbolizes the life breath of the eternal light in everything.

THE HANGED MAN IN MAGICKAL WORK

Energies: Guidance, insight, letting go

Lunar Phases: Full moon, waxing moon, waning moon

The lunar phases are very flexible when using The Hanged Man in magickal workings as this card has a broad range of potential. We can use it either to gain insight or to let go of situations that have bothered us. If you work to gain insight through meditation or the like, use the full moon or waxing moon; remember, you are drawing in. If you are doing meditations to gain large downloads of spiritual guidance, your ideal lunar phase is the full moon, as it's at its highest potential. If you are working with the energies of letting go, you are pushing out, so the waxing moon is the best option.

When picking spellwork and ritual work that works best with The Hanged Man, we are focusing on releasing energy and gaining guidance. This is very much a card of raising our vibrations and accepting guidance. Meditating with this card when doing guided meditation for spirit guides would be appropriate, as would using it as an intentional marker when practicing scrying divination. It helps us seek out information and download it to our brains with an open mind and heart.

We can use The Hanged Man in spell- and ritual-work that involves letting go of situations we no longer have control over. A great example of this would be using The Hanged Man as a symbol of letting go in a fire burning release ritual. We are letting go and releasing energies that no longer serve us. The Hanged Man's presence represents the physical act of allowing ourselves to let go in a purposeful way. Remember that The Hanged Man's hands are behind his back but not clearly bound. He is not forced to let go; he is choosing to let go, just as we are choosing to let go in these rituals.

LETTING GO OF TOXICITY

Letting go of toxic habits and toxic people takes follow-through and won't just happen because of a spell. However, allowing yourself the space to let go is the first step in your journey of recovery. Releasing negativity is sometimes all we need to gently nudge us toward healthier behaviors and surroundings.

Lunar Phases: Dark moon (ideally), waning moon is also fine
Day of the Week: Wednesday
Astrological Moon Phase: Moon in Pisces

INGREDIENTS

- The Hanged Man tarot card
- Flammable poppet (not clay)
- Something flammable to stuff your poppet, such as straw or cotton
- Needle and thread
- Flammable representation of what you are releasing
- Cauldron, fireplace, or bonfire
- Sticks, logs, and your choice of regular fire-starting materials

INSTRUCTIONS

This is a simple spell and a complicated, time-consuming spell all in one. I recommend making a poppet of yourself. To do this, make two gingerbread man shapes out of fabric. Sew the two pieces together and stuff them with flammable material. I recommend enclosing a piece of paper with your name on it or adding some of your hair, fingernail clippings, or the like to really bond you with your poppet.

Bind the flammable representation of what you are releasing to your poppet, just as The Hanged Man's hands are bound behind him. Using needle and thread, sew together the representation and poppet, including the hands, until secure.

If you are using a fireplace or a bonfire, make sure your fire is lit and burning well before beginning this spell. If you are using a cauldron, start a little fire inside it.

Throw your poppet into the fire while repeating the following spell three times:

I let go of the control these bounds have on me.
I release this toxicity from my life.
I will grow and let this be,
No longer causing me strife.
So mote it be.

Let your poppet burn until it is completely gone. Start your next day with a new mindset. Remember, this ritual is only the first step on a long journey. Take steps to better yourself moving forward.

13 DEATH

ZODIAC	Scorpio
RULES	Pluto
ELEMENT	Water
COLOR	Green-blue
AS A YES OR NO QUESTION	No
UPRIGHT	Change, end and beginning, letting go, physical death (incredibly rare), rebirth, transformations, transitions
REVERSED	Inner purging, refusing to let go, resisting change, violent change that is unexpected

We see the Grim Reaper in black armor riding a white horse. The Grim Reaper's suit of armor makes him invulnerable to attack, one of many representations on this card of the inevitability of Death. The original RWS card also shows a king lying dead, a priest praying, and a young maiden and child. The king's death is a reminder that everyone dies: It does not matter how much money or power you have—Death is guaranteed. We are all on a one-way road to the afterlife, whether we are comfortable with that or not. The king's death is also a representation of our choice to either beg for Death not to take us or to accept that Death is inevitable and live our life embracing its truth.

13 DEATH

DEATH'S SYMBOLISM

The black flag the Reaper holds has a white rose on it, representing the mystic rose. This is a biblical symbol for the Virgin Mary, Queen of Heaven and Earth, as well as a symbol for Christ himself. If Christian symbolism does not feel relevant to you, take it as a sign of heaven, the afterlife, and what lies beyond.

The sun is an important symbol. In esoteric teaching, its placement reminds us that although Death is inevitable, the sun will always rise tomorrow. There have been quite a few arguments over whether the sun is setting or rising on this card. We assume that the sun in this card is rising, as it does in traditional occult, since all rivers flow east in esoteric teaching. Therefore, the sun—which appears from the side at which the river flows—must be rising. The Grim Reaper is also moving toward the east. But you can choose to see it either way; the two options are manifestations of the same force. The setting sun tells us that death is upon us, and it is the end. The rising sun tells us of cycles and a transformation into a new day.

DEATH IN MAGICKAL WORK

Energies: New beginnings, letting go, transformation
Lunar Phase: New moon

Death signifies change and transformation in both a forceful way and a positive way. Much like physical death, it brings a new chapter to our lives. It is sudden, permanent, and transformative. Think of the cycle of life: When an animal dies in the woods, new plant life flourishes. It is a dramatic change, but it results in a new, healthy, growing future. Because of this, we will always work with Death during the new moon. It is the beginning of the new lunar cycle, one that allows us to bring in energies that contribute to new beginnings.

When working with the Death card, we are working on positive transformation and a new beginning for ourselves. This could be anything from transitioning gracefully from college to the workforce to settling down with a permanent partner. We are transforming our personal life for the better. What is it that needs change for you? New chapters sometimes call for big and effective boosts of energy to see us through to success. Use Death to draw in phoenix-like energy. We are at the end of the road and the end of a life cycle.

Death can also be seen as having the same energy of letting go as The Hanged Man. Death, in life, is inevitable; no one is free from its cold grasp. When using Death in our spellwork, we may find ourselves needing to capture that energy of truth and acceptance. If we can accept a situation for what it is, then we can let go and move on.

CALLING A NEW BEGINNING

We often find ourselves in situations that call for a fresh start but need a kick to get going. This spell is great to use when you're on the cusp of profound change. You've made the conscious decision to put your life in a new direction; the universe just needs to align in your favor. I wouldn't recommend using this for a love spell or with a specific person. Instead, we are focusing on closing one chapter of our lives and beginning anew. Keep your heart open and be willing to accept this new change for the better.

Lunar Phase: New moon
Day of the Week: Sunday
Astrological Moon Phase: Moon in Pisces

INGREDIENTS
- Black candle
- Green candle
- White candle
- Strawberry incense
- The Death tarot card
- Offerings specific and appropriate to your deity or spirits

INSTRUCTIONS
Light the black candle and take a few moments to ground yourself. Especially when calling in such shifts in our life, grounding is incredibly important. After you feel adequately grounded, light the two remaining candles and your incense. Place your Death card before you. Take a few moments here to meditate on what this path shift will do for you. Don't spend too much time focusing on what you want it to look like; remember to keep an open heart and an open mind. When you are ready, repeat two times:

> Life is an ever-evolving path, changing with each step of my journey.
> This road has come to an end.
> I am ready to accept and embrace the new path before me.
> I call upon the energies of the Death card to aid me in my
>   new chapter.
> I release the energies that no longer serve me.
> A new journey opens for me, allowing me to become who
>   I want to be.

Allow the candles to burn out completely, keeping the Death card in plain sight. Leave offerings on your altar and allow the universe to work. Go into this with an open heart; it may take time, but the new path will open. Don't be afraid to step onto it.

14 TEMPERANCE

ZODIAC	Sagittarius
RULES	Jupiter
ELEMENT	Fire
COLOR	Blue
AS A YES OR NO QUESTION	Yes
UPRIGHT	Abstinence, balance, blending, doctors, flow, healers, karma, moderation, opposites, patience, purpose, recovery, self-control
REVERSED	Addictions, disharmony, excess, imbalances, irritability, need for re-alignment, restlessness, unhealthiness

Historically, the word *temperance* refers to abstaining from alcoholic drinks. When we look at the fifteenth card of the Major Arcana, Temperance, we see the act of diluting water with wine. We see a winged angel of no particular gender (although some sources do identify this angel as Michael). The angel holds two cups, moving the water and wine between them. Although this is not necessarily abstaining from drinking, it reflects the conscious choice to have less to maintain control over the mind and body. The two cups are also a nod to the balance between opposites: We do not need wine, though we do need water. We can have both if we balance the two correctly.

14 TEMPERANCE

TEMPERANCE'S SYMBOLISM

In the RWS Temperance card, the angel's gown shows a triangle within a square, a symbol that has two meanings. First, it is the reason why some call this angel Michael. This triangle within the square is a Tetragrammaton, which is a reference to God, of whom Michael is the angelic representation. Second, this symbol represents the spiritual aspects of ourselves that remain within the material world.

As Temperance represents our need for balance and control over a situation, the theme of balance repeats itself heavily. This angel is shown with one foot in the water, one on land. This act of touching both the land and the water symbolizes harmony between our emotions and our bodies. The pool of water represents our subconscious or emotions, and if we look closely, we can see that the water is flowing, suggesting that this subconscious is active and accessible. The foot on land suggests that we can transform the ideas we receive from our subconscious into tangible, real-world concepts for practical use.

Finally, small and in the distance, we see mountains. These mountains represent both the structural ability to find the balance this card seeks and the birth of new ideas. The connections between the land and water, the subconscious and the material world, have worked. New ideas are forming in perfect harmony.

TEMPERANCE IN MAGICKAL WORK

Energies: Sobriety, self-control, patience, communication

Lunar Phases: Full moon, waning moon, dark moon

With the Temperance card, we are looking heavily at magick that deals with abstinence and sobriety. Addiction is something more of us suffer from than we often realize, and it comes in a variety of forms. Sobriety can look like abstinence from alcohol or drugs, but it can also be sobering to cut ourselves off from toxic people or habits. Because of this, we are looking to work with lunar phases that deal with pushing out— waning and dark moons. We are trying to abstain from toxic behaviors, thought patterns, and people. Using magick that pushes these types of energies out of our life calls for lunar phases that match.

You can also use Temperance to get the flow of conversation back up and running through magick. Although Temperance is a card of patience, the symbolic flowing of two cups can spark or reignite a conversation between two people. If, for example, you and a friend had a falling out and you'd like to find the words to speak to them, Temperance can help. Water and wine mixing together, as we have seen, is by no means outside the realm of possibility. Two people can get together again too. This is not a card I would recommend for love spells; it is simply to get speech and words to flow.

WASHING AWAY THE HABITS

Ritual baths are an amazing form of magick combined with consequential self-care. When we find ourselves realizing that we hold bad habits, this simple ritual bath is a great first step in a new direction. This ritual bath is essential oil-heavy, and therefore, you should be sure you are not allergic to any of these essential oils before soaking your body in them. Make substitutes with dried herbs if this is the case, making the bath gentler on your skin.

Lunar Phase: New moon
Day of the Week: Sunday
Astrological Moon Phase: New moon in Scorpio

INGREDIENTS

- ½ cup (200 g) bath salts, Epsom salts, or Himalayan salts
- 10 drops clary sage essential oil
- 10 drops lavender essential oil
- 5 drops lemongrass essential oil
- 5 drops rosemary essential oil
- 5 drops frankincense essential oil (optional)
- The Temperance tarot card

INSTRUCTIONS

Before beginning, take a few moments to come up with a mantra to repeat to yourself in the tub. This could be as simple as "I will make better choices." For this ritual bath, bad habits could include a broad range of behaviors, so take a moment to come up with a mantra that pertains to you and your circumstance.

Combine the salts with the oils (or herbs) and draw a hot bath, adding in the mixture when the bath is full. Either place the Temperance card where you can easily see it, or simply keep the symbolism and imagery in your mind for the next part.

Get in the bath, inhale the fragrance deeply, and visualize two cups. One cup represents your negative habits, the other is positive energy. Imagine yourself diluting your bad habits with positive energy. Imagine yourself making the conscious choice to forbid the bad habits from becoming so prominent in your situation. Remain in the bath until it begins to cool. Before you leave, say your mantra once more, from the beginning. Then leave the bath, ready to dilute your habits.

15 THE DEVIL

ZODIAC	Capricorn
RULES	Saturn
ELEMENT	Earth
COLOR	Violet or black
AS A YES OR NO QUESTION	No
UPRIGHT	Abuse, addiction, BDSM, denial, deviancy, fear, hate, materialism, punishment, restriction, self-infliction, sexuality, shackles, shadow self, temptation
REVERSED	Detachment, discipline, freedom, hard work, recovery, releasing of restraints, unawareness of shackles

We see a devil figure perched on a black box, a box filled with memories and potential. We cannot see what is inside this box, only the male and female figures who are chained to it. Although they are unable to see the full potential of what is inside the box, they cannot let go of it either. The chains on this box represent our limits to mortality. We are bound by self-inflicted constraints and the universal truth that we will not live forever, unlike this devil figure.

15 THE DEVIL

THE DEVIL'S SYMBOLISM

A large devil-like or demonic figure with horns sits perched on a black box in the RWS tarot card. His horns represent his animalistic nature and the stubbornness that comes with it, mirrored in his goat legs. He also has two large bat wings, which, among other things, represent the nature of the bat. Bats are nocturnal animals who feast in the darkness. They have a deep association with things that go bump in the night, including vampires—blood-sucking monsters who appear in pop culture to scare us. The bat wings can also suggest that darkness and the fear that comes with it have taken over. The Devil is fat, overindulging on food, wine, and sex. He embodies gluttony, one of the seven deadly sins. Above his head, we see an inverted pentagram. Although this symbol has many meanings, in this case, we are looking at its direct association to The Devil.

The nooses around the couple's necks look loose enough to take off, yet neither the man nor the woman seems inclined to remove their bondage. This gives the impression that they are there of their own free will. This bondage situation is one they can walk away from, but greed or fear keeps them restrained.

Grapes grow from the woman's tail, representing sexuality, sensuality, and lust. Meanwhile, the man's tail is a grape leaf that has turned to flame, like The Devil's torch. The man and woman also have horns. The longer they stay with The Devil, the more they become creatures of the night, just like him.

THE DEVIL IN MAGICKAL WORK

Energies: Sexuality, impotence, addiction, recognizing and releasing obstacles

Lunar Phase: Any

When working with The Devil, we are almost always looking at sexual problems, addictions, or releasing addictions in our life. The lunar phases involved are quite flexible because sexuality-based spellwork is also very flexible.

To work with sex magick that involves drawing in your sexuality and power, use a strong moon such as the full moon. This way, you can use your sexuality at the highest lunar phase to draw in energies you want to use in your spellwork. When working with The Devil card, we might find ourselves using sex magick as a means of control and taking back control in our lives. As The Devil deals heavily with control, either a lack thereof or a choice to be controlled, we can use it as a form of ritualistic sex magick for owning our personal power.

The Devil's connection with sexuality can also go in another direction. When we struggle with sexual issues, such as impotence or low libidos, we can use The Devil as a symbolic tool for working with counteracting magick. This would be between two consenting parties who are willing to acknowledge the sexual problems before them and want to tackle those problems as a team. To use The Devil for this form of magick, consider pairing it with the waning or dark moon. We are releasing those energies that The Devil is holding onto so tightly, allowing us to move forward with less or no sexual anxiety.

CONSENTING SEXUAL BOOST

Use this simple spell between two consenting adults to take on sexual power and increase libido. Although some people argue that you can perform a sex spell on someone without their knowledge, I do not recommend it. There are a variety of issues that can go wrong with this spell if the other person is not consenting, including them being too attached. This is a great spell to use in consenting BDSM relationships, as one person will always be the dominant party.

Lunar Phase: Full moon
Day of the Week: Friday
Astrological Moon Phase: Moon in Scorpio

INGREDIENTS
- Plate
- Sugar
- Cayenne pepper
- High John oil
- Red candle and snuffer
- The Devil tarot card

INSTRUCTIONS
On a plate, combine equal parts sugar and cayenne pepper. Drizzle High John oil over the mixture until it's evenly spread. It does not need to completely cover the plate. Carve your sexual partner's name into the red candle or write it on the glass, depending on the kind of candle you have chosen to work with.

Place The Devil card underneath the plate and place both underneath the bed that the two of you will be sharing for this sexual encounter. Leave the candle burning on the bedside table throughout. This pairing will promote sexuality, dominance, and passion. Leave the candle burning until you are done, safely extinguishing it with a snuffer; do not blow out this candle.

16 THE TOWER

ZODIAC	Aries
RULES	Mars
ELEMENT	Fire
COLOR	Red
AS A YES OR NO QUESTION	No
UPRIGHT	Destruction, chaos, suffering, negative shift or change, false beliefs, lies, sudden change, upheaval, awakening, forced change
REVERSED	Fear of change, delayed danger, avoiding disaster, preparing for inevitable chaos, avoiding taking risks

We see two figures falling from The Tower to their destruction by their own hands. There is no person atop this tower who has pushed them from great heights; instead, they have leapt to their deaths. The figures appear to be the king and queen of this royal tower. Much like The Death card, this card is a reminder that even with ultimate power, we can fall perilously by our own hand. Falling is a befitting way to convey the absolute loss of control. No railing or net will catch this king and queen.

16 THE TOWER

THE TOWER'S SYMBOLISM

A tower, for which this card is named, imposes on the skyline, jutting up from the ground below. Falling from its peaks we see a crown, reminding us that this is a royal tower. If we look closely, we see that The Tower sits atop a rocky mountain. This is a reflection of man's conquering nature and a reminder that nature always wins. This man versus nature imagery is seen again in the fire and the lightning surrounding the falling tower.

Fire is typically a very aggressive symbol. It is uncontrollable; although it can be quelled, its nature cannot be tamed. It will obliterate everything in its path, leaving little of the original landscape. In this case, The Tower appears to be made of stone or cement, not something easily destroyed by fire. But the chaos that comes with it, even if the structure is sturdy, remains the same. Lightning has long been seen as a direct message of destruction from God. It is a powerful message of truth emanating from our highest source, forcing us to conduct a reality check. It is a universal symbol of humbling and reality. In nature, we are only safe from lightning's electric touch when protected by a grounded object such as a house or tree.

THE TOWER IN MAGICKAL WORK

Energies: Radical change, awakenings
Lunar Phases: Full moon, new moon

The Tower is best used in magick that requires uncomfortable, radical change. Sometimes the things that are best for us are not the most comfortable choice for us to make. They require massive overhauls and painful separations. The Tower is best paired with the new moon and the full moon. The moon is at its most powerful phase during the full moon, allowing us to tap into its full lunar energies, which I recommend when enacting radical change. The new moon is also a viable source of lunar energies, as its associations are with new beginnings and fresh starts. Although it may not hold the highest potential of the lunar phases, it is aligned so perfectly that I would argue it is just as good as the full moon.

Although The Tower as a tarot card can signify some negativity, for magickal purposes we recognize that negativity and use it to our benefit to shift the narrative. When our situation requires a massive upheaval and we recognize the problem, ritualistic witchcraft is our solution. You must accept that you need the change before you can use magick as a solution.

Radical changes that may call for the use of The Tower can include finding the strength to leave an abusive partner, a drastic weight loss journey (for the betterment of your health), embarking on a new career or educational journey, and even starting a journey involving mental health help. These are all terrifying if you've never done them before, yet they put us in a position of potentially being far healthier and happier. When we have the self-awareness that our life needs a drastic change, we call on the energies of The Tower to aid us in taking the first step to a happier life.

TIME FOR A CHANGE

This simple spell is easy to do and a constant reminder of what we are promising ourselves we will achieve. Although we start this spell over a seven-day course, part of it remains on our altar until our intuition tells us we can let it go. Because everyone's journey is different, this could last for a month, or it could last for five years. It's really down to you! There is no wrong answer.

Lunar Phase: Full moon
Day of the Week: Thursday
Astrological Moon Phase: Moon in Scorpio

INGREDIENTS
- The Tower tarot card
- Pen
- Paper
- Envelope
- Cinnamon and frankincense incense

INSTRUCTIONS
This is a relatively simple spell as it is intended just to reinforce a decision we have already made. To begin, before going to bed, write down where you want to be. What does this radical change do for you? What does your year ahead look like? How about the one after that? Focus on why this is important and what parts of your daily life you need to shed to make it a reality.

After you have written down your intentions and everything that this radical upheaval means to you, place it in your envelope with The Tower card. Hold it in your hand for a moment. Meditate on the idea of yourself throwing the energies that hold you back from your next chapter out of your own tower. Light the incense before going to bed for the night and place your envelope under your pillow.

Sleep with your envelope under your bed for seven nights. You can return The Tower card back to its deck but keep the envelope of writing on your altar until it feels right to discard it.

17 THE STAR

ZODIAC	Aquarius
RULES	Pluto
ELEMENT	Air
COLOR	Violet and blue
AS A YES OR NO QUESTION	Yes
UPRIGHT	Faith, hope, possibilities, destiny, happiness, spirituality, not giving up, optimism, help, spiritual guide, illumination, rejuvenation, love, peace, hope
REVERSED	Hope lost, guilt, sexual guilt, low self-esteem, negativity, despair

A naked woman pours water out of her pitchers under starlight. She could be in the middle of bathing or cleaning up after having bathed herself under the night sky. The water pitchers are often thought to represent pouring Water of Life from two great ewers, irrigating sea and land. Ground rises behind the woman, and on the right a bird alights on a shrub or tree. In tarot, the woman's nakedness is a reminder of her truth. She is comfortable with who she is and doesn't need to hide herself in any capacity. Her figure represents eternal youth and beauty.

17 THE STAR

THE STAR'S SYMBOLISM

In the sky above the woman, we see seven eight-pointed stars
surrounding a greater, more radiant star, also with eight points.
The Star has long been recognized as a symbol of guidance, whether
that means the wise men being led to the Christ child or following the
North Star to find your way home. A great star in the sky is our opening
to the cosmos, a divine oracle. The Star's presence over the maiden's
head shows us her higher level of consciousness, calling us back to the
symbolism of her nudity—she has nothing to hide because she always
knows exactly where she is going.

Seven, the number of stars surrounding the great star, is also the
number of prime chakras, and it is thought to be a symbol of balanced
health. The eight-pointed star may also represent Venus, the evening
star. This symbolism reinforces some of the upright energy of this card's
meanings of love, peace, and hope.

Finally, the small red bird on the RWS card is a symbol of hope,
illuminations, higher vibrations, and aspirations. Birds living both on
land and in the skies represent our ability to lift ourselves up. When we
view ourselves as the bird, we can see ourselves lifted of our burdens, our
spirits flying free above mundane modern restrictions and the confines
we place upon ourselves.

THE STAR IN MAGICKAL WORK

Energies: Happiness, emotional health, luck

Lunar Phases: Flexible, depending on spellwork

The Star's energy of optimism and hope is one that so many of us need in dark times. When we find ourselves falling down a rabbit hole of negativity, it's easy to become trapped. But doing some spellwork accompanied by real-life action can put us on the right track to digging ourselves out of these depressive or down patches—bettering ourselves, our situations, and our mental health. The Star is good to use when you want to put yourself on a better path, improving your situation and well-being.

When working with The Star, we are working with energies that either draw good fortune our way or push out the negative energies we are harboring. This optimistic open-endedness makes The Star card flexible with lunar phases; the best lunar phase to use depends on the energies we want to work with. If, for example, you are in a depressive or down patch in your life and find yourself wanting to push out the negativity, work with the waning moon or the dark moon. But if you just need a bit of luck and positive fortune coming your way, work with the full or waxing moon.

RELEASING HEARTBREAK POTION

This fairly simple, straightforward ritual can help one get over heartbreak of any nature. When using it, we are deciding to look forward and release the past. You can use this potion to get over romantic heartbreak, but it also works for heartbreak over any form of loss, not just romantic loss. Consider The Star's optimism and what possibilities may lay ahead.

Lunar Phase: Waning moon
Day of the Week: Sunday
Astrological Moon Phase: Moon in Cancer

INGREDIENTS
- Small jar with a lid
- Red wine
- 2 teaspoons (1.3 g) lemon balm
- 2 teaspoons (3 g) skullcap
- Rose quartz (optional)
- The Star tarot card

INSTRUCTIONS
Combine red wine, lemon balm, and skullcap in the jar. Add rose quartz, if using. Cover the jar with the lid and leave it in the moonlight overnight.

The next day, strain the herbs and rose quartz from your wine. Place The Star card on your altar and take a moment to toast to the future. You may give yourself a prepared speech or simply mentally acknowledge your optimistic future ahead. Toast to The Star and all its possibility.

18 THE MOON

ZODIAC	Pisces
RULES	Jupiter and Neptune
ELEMENT	Water
COLOR	Violet-red
AS A YES OR NO QUESTION	No
UPRIGHT	Illusions, delusions, fantasy, secrets, dreams, sleep, intuition, influence, confusion, emotion, cycles
REVERSED	Deception, shadows, fear, moodiness, pressure, anxiety, fear-based delusions

The low-hanging moon is in no particular phase; instead we see it in a few phases at once: a crescent moon, a half moon, and a full moon. The half moon contains the profile of a sleeping face. Sleep is where the subconscious, psychic prophecies, and our wildest imaginations come to life. In sleep, we leave our physical bodies and open our minds to boundless possibility and imaginative spirit. This moon hangs between two pillar-like towers, its light shining on everything we see in the card. The towers, firstly phallic symbols, are a nod to our base primal nature. They also represent a comfortable life inside, away from the wild animals we see drawn to The Moon.

THE MOON'S SYMBOLISM

The Moon's presence has affected everything on this card that is alive. We see a domesticated dog and a wolf howl at The Moon as a lobster comes out of a small pool of water. All three are responding to the presence of The Moon. The wolf and the dog represent two facets of our response to this unreachable presence in the sky: the urge to chase The Moon and the difficulty of solving the puzzle of reaching it. Both the dog and the wolf bark at what they can't reach—something we all do from time to time via anxiety or mood swings. They're longing for an untouchable object, which represents our own need to long for *something*. Without desire, tangible or otherwise, we become submissive, passive, and lifeless. The lobster's emergence from the depths below represents coming out of the dark and fully realizing our potential. It is a longstanding symbol of untapped psychic power.

Although no actual moon can perform this level of illumination, The Moon shines so brightly that it casts no shadows. This brightly lit scene transverses between the water, grasses, and mountains, with only a path connecting all three. This path leading toward The Moon from the water suggests that it leads us to a land of intuition and creativity.

THE MOON IN MAGICKAL WORK

Energies: Psychic awareness, nightmares, illusions, glamour magick

Lunar Phase: Any

We have a rare opportunity with this card; we can use The Moon whenever we want, regardless of intention. The card itself holds the images of several lunar phases, thereby opening the door for us to work with it during any lunar phase.

The Moon is also a very flexible card in terms of magickal uses. Because The Moon is so heavily connected with sleep, intuition, and illusions, it opens us up for a wide range of magickal possibilities. The Moon's connection with psychic awareness brings us way back to The High Priestess's Prophetic Dream Spell. The Moon can be used interchangeably with The High Priestess in this spell.

The Moon's deep connection to sleep also makes it perfect to pair with nightmare wards. Consider how The Moon affects a pile of laundry at night. In the dark, this laundry could look menacing; however, the light of The Moon reminds us of the laundry pile. Nightmare wards, when working with this card, can emulate the same energy. The Moon provides a way to consciously remind yourself, even in dreamland, that you are in fact dreaming and none of it is real.

The Moon's connection with illusions also brings us to a lesser-discussed form of magick: glamour magick. We can use The Moon's energy to aid us in charming jewelry, makeup, a hair tie, or the like to help us appear confident and graceful. Although glamour magick will never turn your hair blonde, like in the movie *The Craft*, it can give you that same confidence to carry yourself in a room in such a way that draws in nothing but positive attention.

FULL NIGHT'S REST OIL

Nightmares are something so many of us struggle with! They can keep you up all night, ruining the following day. Using The Moon tarot card, we can consciously separate dreamland and reality. Combining this oil with the intention of lucid dreaming, we can separate reality from dreams and potentially change the narrative of our dreams. Although this is a practice, one that takes more than a single spell, it can be a step toward warding off nightmares and redirecting them when they do appear.

Lunar Phase: Any, preferably waning moon
Day of the Week: Wednesday
Astrological Moon Phase: Moon in Pisces

INGREDIENTS
- Lavender
- Hyacinth
- Mimosa
- Mugwort
- St John's Wort
- Poppy seed
- Carrier oil of choice
- Jar for oil, preferably with dropper top (A dropper top is own preference in application, but the vessel itself is not what's most important here)
- The Moon tarot card

INSTRUCTIONS
Make the oil by combining the dried herbs with the carrier oil in a jar.

Place The Moon card in a clear and visible place on your altar. Holding your fresh oil mixture in hand, close your eyes and visualize the scene. Visualize yourself being the dog or the wolf. You are barking at this moon. Shifting the narrative, you begin to realize that you are barking at The Moon. You release your illusion and go back to less hysteric reactions.

Place the oil outside or on a windowsill that gets sunlight. Arrange The Moon card next to or underneath it. Allow the mixture to sit in the sunlit area for one week. Doing this will allow your herbs to seep into the oil.

Then, before going to bed, put some oil on your wrists and temples. Take a brief moment while doing this to remind yourself of the meditation you did at the beginning of creating your oil. Set the intention that your illusions will lift and you will see the reality of the situation.

19 THE SUN

ZODIAC	Leo
RULES	Sun
ELEMENT	Fire
COLOR	Orange
AS A YES OR NO QUESTION	Strong yes
UPRIGHT	Positivity, fulfillment, clarity, clear view, warmth, radiance, Summer, life, vitality, energy, good, success, rewards
REVERSED	Feeling burnt out, sunburn, depression, clouds, sadness, moodiness

The Sun, our nearest star in terms of astronomy, brings life to our entire planet. Without The Sun, we would have no crops, no lights, and no warmth to sustain our existence. In tarot, The Sun brings the same joy, warmth, and radiance to the Major Arcana. The image on The Sun card appears to take place in the dead of Summer, considering the row of sunflowers, The Sun's central position and strong rays, and the clear sky. If we push it further, this card suggests that it may be Midsummer, the longest and brightest day of the year.

19 THE SUN

THE SUN'S SYMBOLISM

In the RWS tarot card, a small child with golden hair rides a horse in the nude. Both the child and the white horse are a symbol of purity and innocence. The small child waves a red flag, which mirrors the energy of Summer—passion and vibrance. Red is also the shortest wavelength, which reinforces the child's youthfulness.

If we look closely, we can see that the sunflowers face forward, toward the small child, not The Sun. This suggests that the child carries their own light inside of them. This light shines so brightly that even the flowers follow them. Sunflowers traditionally symbolize adoration and loyalty, which are strongly mirrored in their adoration of this small child. Every part of this card basks in The Sun's life-giving rays. It exudes a joyous feeling, without much consideration of the symbolism within the card, and therefore is one of the few cards in the Majors that requires little breakdown.

THE SUN IN MAGICKAL WORK

Energies: Happiness, success, luck

Lunar Phase: Waxing moon

As The Sun is all about the Summer's warm radiance and the happiness that vitamin D brings into our life, we will always be working with the waxing moon when using this card. The waxing moon works with energies that draw energy into our life.

When using The Sun, we are focusing on drawing the energies of happiness, success, and luck, so I would almost always recommend working with The Sun on a Thursday. Although this isn't always going to run true, Thursdays and The Sun card go hand in hand in my experience. Alternatively, as Sundays are associated with The Sun, the two are also an obvious pairing.

Magickally, The Sun partners best with friendship spells, love spells, and general happiness spells for consenting parties. In this case, you would take a relationship between two consenting parties that is already strong and bond it even further. A great example of this would be adapting a pagan handfasting ceremony into a personal bonding ceremony between partners in the privacy of their own home.

We can also pair The Sun with magick to bring happiness and luck. If you plan on gambling, you could use The Sun's warm and enchanting energy to draw luck or good fortune your way. When we are financially secure, we can find happiness much more easily, assuming the financial security that this card may bring comes with a similar workload. I would argue for using this card during times where you need a little luck at work, for a role, or in a competitive interviewing process. Remember the child's radiance from within; honing this energy to your advantage and luck is a logical connection!

LUCK ATTRACTION

Incense is a simple yet effective way to draw the energies we are working with toward us. As a common offering in magick, its smoke also suffumigates your home while adding intention to the space. This simple incense powder is easy to make and easy to use, drawing in luck, success, prosperity, and happiness.

Lunar Phases: Waxing moon, full moon
Day of the Week: Thursday
Astrological Moon Phase: Moon in Leo

INGREDIENTS
- Nutmeg
- Bayberry
- Grains of paradise
- Buckeye nuts
- Bay leaves
- Mortar and pestle
- Charcoal tablets
- Cauldron or firesafe container
- The Sun tarot card

INSTRUCTIONS
Grind together the herbs with the mortar and pestle until the mixture becomes a powder. While you do, take the time to focus on your intentions. Homemade incense is always the most powerful because we can focus in on our exact intentions while making it.

Light a charcoal tablet and place it into your cauldron. Set The Sun card beside the cauldron where it is visible. Sprinkling the powdered incense onto the lit charcoal tablet, recite the following spell:

Warm and radiant Sun,
I give you this token,
Grant me luck as this spell is spoken,
Please send me luck in a positive way.
May The Sun shine on me,
Each and every day.

You can repeat this spell and incense-burning as often as your intuition deems necessary. The smoke from the incense will draw in the energies discussed above, so use it as needed.

20 JUDGMENT

ZODIAC	Scorpio
RULES	Pluto
ELEMENT	Fire
COLOR	Red
AS A YES OR NO QUESTION	Yes, but don't trust your judgment
UPRIGHT	Self-realization, forgiveness, rebirth, renewal, resurrection, past, karma, choices, regret, redemption
REVERSED	Self-doubt, lack of self-awareness, self-loathing, pity, anxiety, fear, the unknown, refusal to learn lessons, denial

Judgment's imagery is a representation of the Biblical "judgment day," or the rapture. The rapture is an eschatological concept that the believers of Christ, both dead and alive, will ascend to the heavens at the end of times. On the skyline, we see the archangel Gabriel blowing his trumpet, calling these believers toward him. We see them rising from their graves and ascending to the heavens above.

20 JUDGMENT

JUDGMENT'S SYMBOLISM

If we look closely, we see that the only figure who is completely turned away from us is the child. This suggests "oneness" with everything as well as the child's purity. A child shouldn't fear judgment, as children are innocent. The man and woman at the child's side are not a suggestion of parents, but a suggestion of the conscious and subconscious. The conscious and subconscious blend together, in a complete form, as the child. The figures' gray color, although they rise from their coffins, is not a representation of their being dead. This is instead a color that represents neutrality, as we saw in The Hierophant. The conscious and the subconscious blend together into a neutral gray. In the background of the RWS tarot card is a mirror image of these three figures. This mirror-like effect shows that we can never hide from the things we have done. Even if others are entirely unaware of our actions, we must always look in the mirror, knowing the truth of our actions.

Also in the RWS version, the coffins float in a body of water in front of snow-covered mountains, which, again, represent our subconscious mind. Water is symbolic of the collective consciousness. Water can be contained and separated, but it also forms a whole. It is a reminder of how everything is interconnected.

JUDGMENT IN MAGICKAL WORK

Energies: Letting go, renewal, choices
Lunar Phases: New moon, waning moon

We can use Judgment's energy of allowing ourselves to not only trust, but to let go of our ideas and fears in many forms of magick. When working with the Judgment card, we are almost exclusively going to be using the energies from the new or waning moons. The new moon is ideal if we are trying to start again. The waning moon is a great way to gently push away the negative energies we are holding within that need to be released. With Judgment, never use the dark moon. Although the dark moon also removes blockages and negativity, its extra strength is not gentle. Think of the child's oneness; we are working with gentle guidance. We are allowing ourselves the space to refresh and start again. We are removing energies that are not serving us and starting again fresh-faced and optimistic.

Because of these renewal and releasing energies, Judgment is a great card to partner with spiritual cleansing of any form. We use it to focus on cleansing our mind, body, and/or soul. Judgment is useful when we need to ease up on ourselves as well. We can use it to forgive ourselves for our shortcomings as well as for things we cannot control or change. We often need to release negative self-talk and thoughts of unworthiness. Releasing can come in the form of fire rituals or through affirmation meditations.

PEACE FROM WITHIN

This gradual renewal spell works slowly but effectively. We are looking to purposefully push out the energies we no longer wish to harbor by giving ourselves a spiritual cold shower. We want to invigorate the spirit and allow ourselves the space to release unwanted tensions.

Lunar Phase: Waning moon
Day of the Week: Sunday
Astrological Moon Phase: Moon in Cancer

INGREDIENTS
- The Judgment tarot card
- Red candle
- Black candle
- White candle

INSTRUCTIONS
Find a quiet place to meditate. If you are like me, you may want to bring headphones and a white noise app; I find they help block out the world around me. Choose somewhere you can arrange a mini altar in front of you.

Place the Judgment card in the middle of the mini alter. Place the red candle in front of it. On the left side, place the black candle, which represents the stresses, tensions, and overall negative energies you are harboring. On the right, place the white candle, representing tranquility, peace, and purified emotional state.

Light the black candle and say aloud:

I recognize and release all the stress and tension surrounding me.

Light the white candle and say aloud:

I am choosing peace and tranquility.

Finally, light the red candle and say aloud:

I allow myself to be happy
With who I am
And who I'll be.
With harm to none, so mote it be.

Now, while your candles are burning, take five to twenty minutes to meditate on this. Try to visualize yourself as one of the gray figures following the trumpet call. Picture your own personal rapture, the happy and light version of yourself ascending. Leave the negativity holding you back in your casket. Meditate on this for as long as feels right to you.

THE WORLD

ZODIAC	Libra
RULES	Saturn
ELEMENT	Earth
COLOR	Blue-violet, indigo
AS A YES OR NO QUESTION	Yes
UPRIGHT	Completion, four corners of the globe, journey, trip, success, achievements, awards, end of a cycle, fulfillment
REVERSED	Failure, delays, being held back, lack of recognition, disharmony

Although we see a figure with breasts, this figure is not gendered; they are androgynous and representative of the masculine and feminine energies combining as one. This figure dances in the air, surrounded by a wreath of laurel, a symbol of victory and success. The laurel leaves are bound at the tops and bottoms with red ribbons, symbolizing the never-ending cycle of life. When one journey ends, another begins, and so this cycle repeats until our time here comes to an end.

21 THE WORLD

THE WORLD'S SYMBOLISM

The dancer or figure we see in the center of the card shows us they're living in perfect harmony with the universe. If you look closely at the figure, you may notice the unique crossing of the legs, which is similar to what we saw on The Hanged Man. This 4-shaped configuration represents a crossroads. Unlike in The Hanged Man, however, we are at the crossroads, and we are complete. There is no need to suspend ourselves; we are satisfied with this crossroads and can move forward with enthusiasm and pride.

If we look to the four corners of this card, we see a man, an eagle, a bull, and a lion. These are symbolic of the four elements; the man is air, the eagle is water, the bull is earth, and the lion is fire. If we look at them in terms of the zodiac, we see the four elements represented again, this time in fixed signs. The man is the air sign of Aquarius. Although the eagle is esoterically out of place, his presence is representative of Scorpio, a water sign. The bull is the earth sign of Taurus, and the lion represents the fire sign of Leo.

THE WORLD IN MAGICKAL WORK

Energies: Success, achievement, new chapters

Lunar Phases: New moon, dark moon

As we are working with energies that are associated with new phases in life, the new moon is best for magick involving The World. The new moon's fresh start energies breathe new life into our intentions. Instead of fear of the future, the new moon gives us a warm energy that helps us embrace the next chapter of our lives. The dark moon could also pair well with The World since, like the new moon, it is associated with the end of a chapter. Although the dark moon's presence is more forceful in removing something from our lives, we can also use it as the understanding needed to accept the next chapter. Acknowledging the end allows us to begin again.

When picking spellwork for this card, we are going to be looking at mostly ritual magick that involves accepting and embracing the next chapter of our lives. With this, we are neither calling in nor pushing away anything. Instead, we make the conscious acknowledgment that our next chapter will be positive. Remember, this card has already accepted what's to come of the next chapter; there is nothing holding us back! Using this card as a ritualistic marker in our celebratory success and to make space for our upcoming goals is ideal. The World is useful in new year's goal-making rituals as well as birthday rituals. We are acknowledging the year we have left in the past and setting goals for the year ahead.

MAKE A WISH AN INTENTION

Blowing out birthday candles is in itself a disjointed, pagan-like ritual. You make a wish and symbolically blow out the candles to cement that wish. We use the same energy for this ritual but take it a step further. This personal ritual pushes you to set goals for the year ahead and to allow yourself the space to release the things you don't want to bring into your next year.

Lunar Phase: Any
Day of the Week: Any (your birthday)
Astrological Moon Phase: Any (your birthday)

INGREDIENTS
- The World tarot card
- A sweet of your choice, preferably a cupcake
- Candle
- Pen and paper
- Cauldron or firesafe container

INSTRUCTIONS
Set up your space: Put The World card beneath your sweet and press the candle into the sweet so it sits there on its own.

On the paper, make two lists. The first is of your intentions for the year ahead. Make them statements, not hopeful wishes. For example, you could write, "I will get promoted this year," or, "I will move to my dream city this year." On the second list, write down the negative parts of the year you are leaving behind, which you will release. Again, write these as statements. For example, you could write, "I will no longer bite my nails," or, "I will seek help when I need it."

Light the candle. First, hold your list of energies that no longer serve you. Ignite this list with your candle and place it into your cauldron to burn completely. Then hold your intentions list, close your eyes, and imagine yourself as the figure dancing in the laurel leaves. Pause on the idea of the list of intentions you have made. Then blow out your candle and enjoy your treat. It's your birthday—you earned it! Place the list of the intentions you have set for the year discreetly on your altar, until your next birthday. You can use this each year to revisit the goals you had set the year before.

5

CORRESPONDENCE
IN MAGICK
AND TAROT

Correspondence is the lifeblood of all magick. When we look at correspondences in magick, we are looking at anything—from lunar phases to colors—that is directly correlated to an energy or intention a practitioner may use. Most of these correspondences date back thousands of years, and there is almost always a historical reference as to why we correlate them to the energies we work with today.

When we consider using tarot as a ritual tool, we use the key elements within each card as correspondence. This ranges from the cards' numerological associations to which moon phase works best with the energies each card holds. When we combine these magickal "ingredients" together, we can begin to create our own rituals and spells.

BASIC NUMEROLOGY

Numbers can have significant synchronicities in our lives, and we can therefore apply them to spellwork, including through numerology. The single digit numbers one through nine are the foundation of all numerology. When we have a basic understanding of these numerological energies, we can apply them to tarot, future divinations, spellwork, and so on. Each number has its own associations, strengths, and weaknesses.

Using numerology, we can hone in on the energies of a tarot card to mirror what we are trying to manifest. For example, you could pair the energy of home and stability in the number four with trying to get that apartment you are applying for. If you had a magickal oil, you could use however many drops of oil correspond with the energies that you are working with in your spellwork. Magick is all about correspondence and layering it in the way that is most powerful. Numerology just becomes another layer of that magickal correspondence, if you so choose.

1 One is associated with the ultimate power and with being "one" with the universe. All of nature's primal forces begin with the building blocks of the number one. It is also the number for the self and the confidence that comes with that.

POSITIVE KEYWORDS	Unity, action motivator, leadership, building block, foundations
NEGATIVE KEYWORDS	Ego, domination, hastiness, stubbornness

2 Two is a very important number to pagans, as witchcraft is all about balance. Two can bring the symmetry and balance we focus on. It is often connected with yin and yang or with the polarity of our personalities.

POSITIVE KEYWORDS	Unions, partnerships, flexibility, communication, reason, balance
NEGATIVE KEYWORDS	Nervousness, coyness, depression, overthinking

3 Three is often viewed as a magickal or lucky number. It is connected to the Triple Goddess, or the Maiden/Mother/Crone.

POSITIVE KEYWORDS	Happiness, luck, completion, growth, childbearing, nurture, insight, intuition
NEGATIVE KEYWORDS	Unfinished projects, moodiness, selfishness, lack of direction

4

Four corresponds to the four elements, the cardinal directions, and the four seasons. It is the number of houses, stability, and safety. Remember, a house is made up of four walls.

POSITIVE KEYWORDS	Morals, structure, stability, foundational achievements, family, safety, attention to detail
NEGATIVE KEYWORDS	Being caught up in details, sluggishness, taking things too seriously

5

In paganism, five is associated with the combination of the spirit with the four elements. Five is also associated with the five human senses, our connection to the world around us.

POSITIVE KEYWORDS	Free-thinking, independence, individualism, experience, adventurer, teacher/student, visionary
NEGATIVE KEYWORDS	Unreliability, irresponsibility, inconsistency, self-absorption

6

Six is a solar number associated with the masculine energies of the sun. Because of this, we are looking at energies associated with security, responsibility, and problem-solving.

POSITIVE KEYWORDS	Security, responsibility, problem-solving, life, growth, happiness, humanitarianism
NEGATIVE KEYWORDS	Overwhelmed with responsibilities, struggle to say no, easily stressed, disconnection, submissiveness

7 Seven is the counterpart to six, and it is associated with the moon and feminine energies. It is also considered a lucky number; think lucky number seven at a casino.

POSITIVE KEYWORDS	Luck, intuition, wisdom, divination, goddess, seeker of knowledge, meditation
NEGATIVE KEYWORDS	Secretiveness, malicious motives, inflexibility, unwillingness to learn, poorly divided attention

8 Eight is associated with the eight pagan Sabbats, as well as with Mercury. Because of this connection to Mercury, the number eight is connected to messages from the divine and communications from the otherworld. When rotated horizontally, it transforms into an infinity sign, a symbol of all-knowing and infinite knowledge.

POSITIVE KEYWORDS	Authority, confidence, higher knowledge, completion, potential, exercise of good judgment
NEGATIVE KEYWORDS	Excessive ambition, poor money management, stress, materialism, workaholism

9 Nine is three squared; it is triple the power and luck of the number three. Nine is associated with Goddess energy and personal growth within.

POSITIVE KEYWORDS	Triple Goddess, full moon, growth, personal change, completion of a process, spirituality, wisdom
NEGATIVE KEYWORDS	Restlessness, disconnection, difficulty concentrating

THE FOUR ELEMENTS

Looking back in time, elements were thought to be broken into four major energy categories: air, earth, water, and fire. With the advancement of science, we now know that there are far more than four elements; however, in ritual magick we still work with the original four. Each minor suit of tarot is directly connected to one of these four elements, while the majors vary card to card. As each element is correlated to a different facet of our daily lives, we can look to the Major Arcana and its elemental correspondence to further our magickal workings.

Everything is about correspondence. If your tarot card, for example, is associated with Water, you may find yourself wanting to channel more of that element. Maybe your spellwork has offerings based around Water and an altar setup that is designed around working exclusively with that element. Although this may not always be true, it can open the doors to more creativity and the ability to write stronger spells.

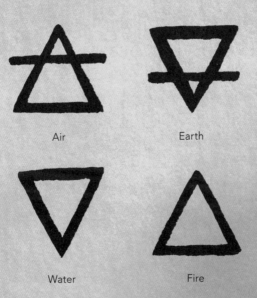

Air

Earth

Water

Fire

I THINK: AIR

Air is one of the only elements that is not tangible. It is something we know is there without having to physically see it. It is ever-changing, and although invisible, it gives us life and is the driving force behind natural factors such as the weather.

Because of this, when we are referring to the magickal marker of Air, our keyword expression is "I think." Thinking is something we know everyone does. We know we think, but we cannot see it in action (unless we make faces when we think). Air energy supports the creation of new ideas and is often associated with traveling and general luck. Although this is a deeply wise element, keep in mind that spells that focus solely on Air energy tend to go as quickly as they come. Air is the **Eastern** marker of the elements of ritual magick and is associated with North in tarot. Because of the winds of change brought forth with the Air element, we will most often perform spellwork involving mental clarity, creativity, and truth.

ENERGIES	Problem-solving, communication, energy, logic, intelligence, honesty, clarity
ALTAR SPACE	Fans, feathers, swords, arrows, pieces of incense, a bunch of fragrant flowers, wands
MAGICKAL CREATURES	Sylphs, griffons, sprites
COLORS	Bright pale, pastel, white, yellow
ZODIAC	Gemini, Libra, Aquarius
SUIT	Swords (some associate with Wands)
MINOR ARCANA	Kings
MAJOR ARCANA	The Fool, The Magician, The Lovers, Justice, The Star
MASCULINE OR FEMININE	Masculine

I AM: EARTH

Earth is the most tangible of all the elements. We can hold it, grow with it, and use it for stability. It is solid, tactile, and safe. Earth, unlike the other three elements, does not change without centuries of time or human effort.

Due to Earth's structure and stability, we use the keywords "I am." There is no questioning with Earth; we are who we are, and there is a safeness in this. Earth matters do not just focus on the tangible—they also focus on matters of the home, such as material resources. Earth's energy supports growth in our home, financially and materialistically. Earth is an element you can count on. When it appears in a reading, we know that this isn't something that will come or go quickly. Earth takes its time. Because of the grounding nature of the Earth element, we will most often perform spellwork involving finances, home life, and stability. Earth is the **Northern** marker in magickal workings and is associated with the East in tarot.

ENERGIES	Money, wealth, home, material goods, health, practical matters, stability, grounding, structure
ALTAR SPACE	Salt, crystals, soil, a pentacle, the altar base itself, coins, cauldrons, flowers
MAGICKAL CREATURES	Land mammals
COLORS	Greens of all shades, brown
ZODIAC	Taurus, Virgo, Capricorn
SUIT	Pentacles
MINOR ARCANA	Pages
MAJOR ARCANA	The Empress, The Hierophant, The Hermit, The Devil, The World
MASCULINE OR FEMININE	Feminine

I FEEL: WATER

Water is fluid and transformative. It can take many forms, from vapor to liquid to solid ice. It's the only element that can take all three of these forms. It can be the soft gentle push of a lake shore or a raging force such as a fast-moving river or the undercurrent of the ocean. Water makes up the majority of our planet. It is adaptive and flowing, and it can be purifying in nature.

Due to Water's ever-changing energy, it is associated closely with our emotions, so the key phrase is "I feel." Our emotions can change with the weather or with hardened experience. Water is also deeply connected with the moon and is often represented as such. Because of Water's connection with intuition and receptivity, use this element with magick involving divination. Water is the **Western** marker in magickal workings as well as in tarot.

ENERGIES	Compassion, emotions, intuition, family, relationships, love, receptivity
ALTAR SPACE	Chalices, cauldrons, a scrying bowl, crystal balls, seashells, driftwood, mirrors
MAGICKAL CREATURES	Nymphs, mermaids, hippocamps
COLORS	Blue, silver, purple
ZODIAC	Cancer, Scorpio, Pisces
SUIT	Cups
MINOR ARCANA	Queens
MAJOR ARCANA	The High Priestess, The Chariot, The Hanged Man, Death, The Moon
MASCULINE OR FEMININE	Feminine

I DO: FIRE

Out of the four elements, fire is the one that can give life as easily as it can take it. Its unpredictable, unwinding energy is representative of the life-giving sun and of destructive forces such as wildfires. It is the only element that cannot be touched without causing harm to the body.

Due to the permanence of Fire's touch, when we think of the element of Fire, we consider the action-based phrase "I do." There is no doubt or pause here, simply the act of moving forward and with gusto. Because of the obvious association between flames and the Fire element, we will most often perform spellwork involving candle magick. Fire is the **Southern** marker in magickal workings as well as in tarot.

ENERGIES	Passion, creativity, life, anger, growth, sexuality, motivation
ALTAR SPACE	Wands, athame, sun symbols, volcanic symbols, candles, a lamp, daggers, swords
MAGICKAL CREATURES	Salamanders, dragons, phoenixes
COLORS	Red, orange, yellow
ZODIAC	Aries, Leo, Sagittarius
SUIT	Wands (Swords)
MINOR ARCANA	Knights
MAJOR ARCANA	The Emperor, Strength, The Wheel of Fortune, Temperance, The Tower, The Sun
MASCULINE OR FEMININE	Masculine

LUNAR PHASES

FULL MOON

This is the most common face of the moon people tend to be comfortable working with. The full moon is considered the time of the month when energy is at its peak and a time marked for esbats. The full moon lasts three days and is associated with the Triple Goddess, so you have a three-day window to celebrate it. The first day is marked as the Maiden, the second as the Mother (when the full moon is at 100 percent), and the third as the Crone. The full moon is a time when we do spellwork intended for specific purposes depending on the monthly energy.

WANING

Waning refers to when the moon's visibility is shrinking. A waning moon begins the day after the Crone full moon and lasts all the way until the crying moon. A waning moon always begins as a gibbous moon (referring to when it is more than half full). Because of the nature of a waning moon shrinking, we use this time to push away or "shrink" things or energies in our life that we don't want. A waning gibbous is seen as a time of gradual pushing, a waning crescent as a time of forceful pushing.

CRYING

The crying moon is the very last sliver of the waning moon right before the dark moon. It is what the new moon would be, only in reverse. Like the new moon it only lasts one day and is often missed and/or forgotten. This is the time of the month with the most negative energy, and therefore, many witches choose not to work with it. Personally, I believe that even if something you are working with is negative, the most important things to consider are your intentions in using it. This is a good time to abruptly end the negative things affecting your life. Knowing this, it is a fine line and a tough balance, so be careful, witches! Traditionally, the crying moon is when most curses start, but, huge disclaimer, please don't go cursing your friends. I want to be well-rounded in what I'm putting out there, so this is simply informative, but let's be responsible.

DARK MOON

This is another lunar phase a lot of witches tend to avoid because of misconceptions about working with negative energy. Witches can use this moon to hex or curse, although due to the Wiccan threefold rule, it is often avoided at all costs. Traditionally, the dark moon is a time of banishing, usually done in a forceful way. This can, however, be a time when we remove things from our lives that no longer serve a purpose to us, such as bad habits. The dark moon holds as much energy as the full moon.

NEW MOON

The new moon is the very first sliver immediately following the dark moon. This is a time for new beginnings, new projects, and fresh starts. This is a time to breathe new life into things. It lasts only one night and is often missed! This is also a great time to cleanse your space, even just by cleaning your house so you can start the month ahead with fresh energy. We can use the new moon to set fresh intentions. Consider honing in on the energy of The Fool card!

WAXING

Last but not least, the waxing moon begins the day after the new moon and lasts all the way until the day before the Maiden full moon. During this time, the moon gives off the illusion of being bigger and brighter than it normally is and has the appearance of growing. As the moon grows, it pulls. Therefore, the waxing moon is an appropriate time to do magick that attracts. The waxing moon is also a slow moon, and it is the best time to do longer spellworking, such as seven-day spells and the like.

6

TAROT
SPREADS

A tarot spread is a formatted layout we use to help us get a card for a specific question or theme. Although tarot spreads are by no means required to read tarot, I prefer them when learning how to interpret the cards. It forces us to look at individual cards for a specific connection between the question and the card drawn. In time you may find that spreads are no longer wanted or necessary, and that is more than valid, but they are a great way to get yourself thinking of the cards in a practical application.

THREE CARD SPREAD VARIATIONS

Three Card Spread is not only the simplest of tarot spreads, it is the most common and the easiest to adjust for your own needs. You can use this adaptable spread for present problems, future outcomes, and insight into the broader picture. By simply focusing on our intention/ question layout while shuffling, we are putting the energy of what we want answered into the cards before even drawing. As we pick our cards, we've already sent the intention out there, and it's up to our intuition or guides to show us the answer.

Here are some examples of card meanings:
- Past/Present/Future
- Situation/Obstacle/Advice
- Mind/Body/Spirit
- Embrace/Accept/Let Go
- Tomorrow/Next Week/Next Month
- Background/Problem/Advice
- Theme of Day/Positive/Obstacle
- Strength/Weakness/Advice
- Option 1 Outcome/Option 2 Outcome/Advice

MAKING MAGICK SPREAD

This spread is both an exercise in learning the magickal energies of tarot and a means of guiding ourselves through our manifestation. It's great to use when you aren't sure how to proceed with an intention but know what your end goal looks like. Before pulling for this spread, take some time to focus on what the end goal for you looks like. Once you've envisioned it, you can begin your normal routine of pulling cards. The card meanings are as follows:

1. Intention (Card connected with the energy you want to work with.)
2. How this energy can help your present situation.
3. What's holding you back from getting there?
4. How to overcome this obstacle.
5. Advice on being realistic through your manifestation process.

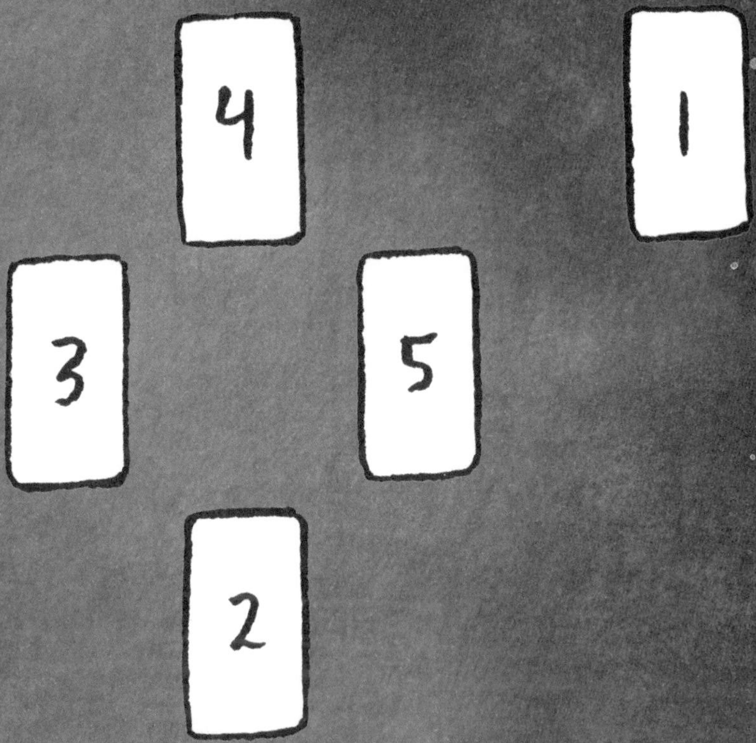
1
2
3
4
5

MONTHLY CHECK-IN SPREAD

A key element to being successful in magick, in my opinion, is being truly honest and realistic with yourself. If you are lying to yourself, how can you expect to grow as a witch? When we allow ourselves this space for listening, we can apply it to improving ourselves. This is not tarot for divination of the future, but it is instead for looking at the present and how best to grow. The card meanings are as follows:

1. Current self
2. What to release from the month left behind
3. Theme of the month ahead
4. What to focus on
5. Biggest obstacle
6. Biggest success
7. Advice

SELF-LOVE SPREAD

Part of finding power from within tarot is finding the power from within ourselves! This self-love spread's main focus is looking inward to remind ourselves of who we are and why we matter. If we can see the positive within ourselves, it's easy to refine our power. Knowing your value becomes knowing your power. The card meanings are as follows:

1. Signifier
2. What is my greatest strength?
3. What is something I don't see in myself but others admire about me?
4. What is something to be proud of?
5. Why do I need to reflect on my positives?
6. What is my greatest personal blockage?
7. What advice do I need to hear right now?

COMING INTO POWER SPREAD

As we are aligning ourselves with tarot and its use to us as a ritual tool, we can use this spread as a guide to the in-between. This is a great cross-over spread, a simple start to building our relationship with our deck, for more than just a divination tool. We are utilizing the four elements we have discussed as well as the fifth element, the Spirit. Each brings a unique part of you into your relationship with witchcraft and your power. The card meanings are as follows:

1. Earth: How can I ground myself better?
2. Air: How are my thoughts perceived by others?
3. Fire: What fuels my goals/dreams/passion?
4. Water: How do I show and receive love/emotions?
5. Spirit: How can I better nourish my soul/spirit?

WORKS CITED

Bartlett, Harriet T. *An Esoteric Reading of Biblical Symbolism.* 1916.
Buckland, Raymond. *Buckland's Complete Book of Witchcraft.*
    Llewellyn Worldwide, 1986.
Chang, T. Susan. *Tarot Correspondences.* Llewellyn Worldwide, 2018.
Chang, T. Susan, and M. M. Meleen. *Tarot Deciphered.* Llewellyn
    Publications, 2021.
Graham, Sasha. *Llewellyn's Complete Book of the Rider-Waite-Smith
    Tarot.* Llewellyn Worldwide, 2018.
Illes, Judika. *Encyclopedia of 5,000 Spells.* Harper Collins, 2011.
—. *The Element Encyclopedia of 1,000 Spells.* HarperCollins UK, 2009.
Kaplan, Stuart R. *Pamela Coleman Smith.* U.S. Games Systems Inc.,
    2018.
Katz, Marcus, and Tali Goodwin. *Secrets of the Waite-Smith Tarot.*
    Llewellyn Worldwide, 2015.
Place, Robert Michael. *The Tarot.* Penguin, 2005.
Waite, A. E. *The Pictorial Key to the Tarot.* Courier Corporation, 2012.
Walker, Barbara G. *The Secrets of the Tarot.* Harper San Francisco, 1984.
Wasserman, James. *Art and Symbols of the Occult.* Inner Traditions,
    1993.

INDEX

ABOUT THE AUTHOR

*"A Witch is a person who has honestly explored their light
and has evolved to celebrate their darkness."*

—DACHA AVELIN

Robyn Valentine was born and raised in the Bay Area of California,
spending the majority of her adult life living in downtown San
Francisco. Robyn and her witchcraft were greatly influenced by both
her mother and grandmother, who identify as witches. Robyn has spent
a great deal of her life studying a wide variety of magick, starting with
the most common path of Wicca but leaving that path shortly after as
she did not agree with some of its fundamental foundations. Currently,
her path is eclectic, and she self-describes as "just your average witch."
She works currently as a professional tarot reader, witchcraft mentor,
blogger, and podcaster. When she is not creating magick, she is
spending time with her husband and two cats.